Managing Online
Instructor Workload

JOSSEY-BASS GUIDES
TO ONLINE TEACHING AND LEARNING

Managing Online Instructor Workload

STRATEGIES FOR FINDING

BALANCE AND SUCCESS

Simone C. O. Conceição
Rosemary M. Lehman

JOSSEY-BASS
A Wiley Imprint
www.josseybass.com

Published by Jossey-Bass
A Wiley Imprint
989 Market Street, San Francisco, CA 94103-1741—www.josseybass.com

Jossey-Bass books and products are available through most bookstores. To contact Jossey-Bass directly call our Customer Care Department within the U.S. at 800-956-7739, outside the U.S. at 317-572-3986, or fax 317-572-4002.

Jossey-Bass also publishes its books in a variety of electronic formats. Some content that appears in print may not be available in electronic books.

Library of Congress Cataloging-in-Publication Data
Conceição, Simone C.O., 1963–
    Managing online instructor workload : strategies for finding balance and success / Simone C.O. Conceição, Rosemary M. Lehman.—1st ed.
      p. cm.—(Jossey-Bass guides to online teaching and learning ; 33)
    Includes bibliographical references and index.
    ISBN 978-0-470-88842-1 (pbk.)
    ISBN 978-1-118-07552-4 (ebk); ISBN 978-1-118-07553-1 (ebk);
    ISBN 978-1-118-07555-5 (ebk)
      1. Distance education—Computer-assisted instruction. 2. Teachers—Workload. I. Lehman, Rosemary M., 1932– II. Title.
    LC5803.C65C66   2011
    371.33'4—dc22

                                             2011012503

Printed in the United States of America

FIRST EDITION

PB Printing   10 9 8 7 6 5 4 3 2 1

CONTENTS

List of Tables and Figures   vii
Preface   ix
About the Authors   xv

ONE Issues and Challenges When Teaching Online   1

Institutional Issues and Challenges   3
Instructional Issues and Challenges   9
Our Study on Instructor Workload When Teaching Online   15
Summary   17

TWO Instructors' Stories for Balancing Workload   19

Co-teaching as a Strategy for Balancing Workload   21
Planning Ahead as a Way to Predict Workload   23
Giving Individual Feedback as a Workload Management Strategy   25
Managing Time, Rather Than Time Managing You   27
Blocking Out Time for the Online Course   28
Teaching Online During Short Terms   30
Using Time Allocation Strategies When Teaching for Multiple Institutions   32
Teaching Online Exclusively from Home   34
Managing Workload Based on Years of Experience   36
Teaching Online for a Variety of Institutions   38
Cohort Program as a Time-Saver   40
Managing Similar Tasks When Designing for Multiple Courses   42

Teaching a Recurring Mixed-Mode Online Course   44

Managing Workload When Current Information Drives Content   45

Summary   48

THREE Looking at Workload from a Design Perspective   **49**

Identifying Course Tasks   51

Why It Is Important to Use an Instructional Design Process   52

Design Framework for Creating a Sense of Presence   54

Using a Template to Manage Tasks and Prioritize Time   61

Summary   62

FOUR Managing Tasks and Prioritizing Time   **63**

Creating a New Online Course   64

Converting a Face-to-Face Course   70

Revising an Existing Online Course   74

Summary   79

FIVE Using Workload Strategies for Maintaining
          Quality of Life   **81**

Design Strategies   82

Support Strategies   86

Teaching Strategies   87

Time Allocation Strategies   90

Summary   94

SIX Final Thoughts and Practical Implications
        for Balancing Workload   **95**

Teaching from an Open Perspective   96

Adapting the Course Design   96

Modifying Workload Strategies   97

Rethinking How to Prioritize Time and Manage Workload   97

Practical Implications for Balancing Workload   99

Glossary   101

References   105

Index   109

LIST OF TABLES AND FIGURES

TABLES

1.1 Institutional Issues and Challenges in Online Teaching   4
1.2 Instructional Issues and Challenges in Online Teaching   9
2.1 Summary of Instructors' Stories for Balancing Workload   21
3.1 Summary of Course Sequence, Types of Tasks,
    and Task Descriptions   53
3.2 Methods for Creating a Course Blueprint   54
3.3 Template for Managing Tasks and Prioritizing Time   62
4.1 Design Elements for a New Online Course   65
4.2 Design Tasks for Building a New Online Course   66
4.3 Managing Tasks and Prioritizing Time for a New
    Online Course   69
4.4 Design Elements for a Converted Online Course   71
4.5 Managing Tasks and Prioritizing Time for a Converted
    Online Course   73
4.6 Design Elements for an Existing Online Course   75
4.7 Managing Tasks and Prioritizing Time for an Existing
    Online Course   78
5.1 Strategies for Balancing Instructor Workload   94
6.1 Rethinking Process for Prioritizing Time and Managing Workload   98

FIGURES

3.1 Framework for Designing Online Courses
    with a Sense of Presence   55

PREFACE

The landscape of higher education is being transformed due to market demands for online learning (Allen & Seaman, 2008). This requires that institutions embrace the concept of online education, acknowledge its benefits and limitations, and act upon it to remain competitive. Today online education is a reality. Its benefits have an impact on institutional growth, and its limitations affect instructor workload. Instructors feel pressured to move their courses online, lack an awareness of what is involved in online instruction, and are unprepared to teach in the online environment. For these reasons, it is evident that administrators and instructors need to take action at the institutional and instructional levels to overcome these limitations.

Institutions have the responsibility to provide instructors with administrative, monetary, and technical support to compete in times of change. To survive in this landscape, instructors must be open to new opportunities and widen their perspectives. To teach in this landscape, they need to take a fresh look at their practice, adapt their course design, modify their teaching strategies, and rethink the ways in which they prioritize and manage their workload.

The view that instructors can take their face-to-face courses and transfer them to the online environment is a common one. However, this is misleading (Carroll-Barefield, Smith, Prince, & Campbell, 2005). Effective online instruction calls for an understanding of the online teaching and learning environment, planning, and intentional design for online offerings (Lehman & Conceição, 2010). Designing, delivering, and evaluating online instruction demand a distinctive type of management when compared to face-to-face instruction. Therefore, managing the online teaching workload has become a concern for both new and experienced instructors.

Information on workload management when teaching online has been meager. Most information is either anecdotal or based on nonempirical studies. In this book we address workload management from an instructor's perspective, drawing on findings from a study we conducted with higher education online instructors and on our own experiences.

THE FOCUS OF THIS BOOK

This book focuses on the strategies instructors use to manage their workload when teaching online. We examine the issues and challenges of online teaching from institutional and instructional standpoints and discuss how they can be recognized and addressed. Further, we relate stories of instructors in different teaching positions and present comprehensive accounts of the strategies they use to manage workload. Based on our study findings and previous work, we explain how to determine appropriate course tasks for online teaching and ways in which these tasks can be accomplished within an instructional design framework. Using three case examples of a new online course, a course converted from face-to-face to online, and an existing online course, we describe how instructors manage tasks and prioritize time for different types of online courses. Finally, we believe that the major concern when dealing with workload is maintaining quality of life, and this book provides a number of strategies to manage workload and prioritize time in order to find balance and success.

WHO CAN BENEFIT FROM THIS BOOK

This book offers instructors, instructional designers, practitioners, and administrators the most current strategies to balance workload when teaching online. Instructors in any position at an educational organization, who are either new to or experienced with online teaching, may use this book. For new instructors, this book can serve as a framework and a guide for designing and delivering online instruction. Experienced instructors can use this book as a way to reflect on their current practice in teaching online and revisit and refine their strategies for more efficient and effective instruction.

Instructional designers can use this book as a guide to help instructors succeed in the online environment. Practitioners who work with programs in organizations or as consultants may use this book as a resource when developing or administering programs, or assisting instructors with creating and delivering courses. Administrators will find this book valuable when establishing, maintaining, and sustaining online offerings in educational institutions and considering issues and challenges instructors face when teaching online.

HOW THIS BOOK IS ORGANIZED

The aim of *Managing Online Instructor Workload: Strategies for Finding Balance and Success* is to provide sound strategies based on research and practical experience. In Chapter One, Issues and Challenges When Teaching Online, we address institutional and instructional issues and challenges of workload management in higher education, and examine their consequences in regard to navigating the new higher education landscape. Also, we describe the study we conducted as a preparation for writing this book and present the major study findings. Each chapter starts with a relevant quote from a study participant that relates to that chapter's content.

In Chapter Two, Instructors' Stories for Balancing Workload, we share comprehensive accounts from individuals who work in a variety of disciplines in different types of institutions, hold various position ranks, teach at the undergraduate and graduate levels, and have diverse experiences with online teaching. The focus of these in-depth stories is on workload strategies and approaches that most concern instructors who teach online.

In Chapter Three, Looking at Workload from a Design Perspective, we discuss the types of course tasks that are suitable for online instruction and explore how an instructor can accomplish these tasks within a design framework. We further explain why it is important to use a systematic approach for designing online instruction and suggest a framework as a guide for designing online courses. We end this chapter by providing a template for managing tasks and prioritizing time.

In Chapter Four, Managing Tasks and Prioritizing Time, we use the template introduced in Chapter Three to describe three ways to design and deliver an online course based on its type. These three types focus on developing a new online course, adapting a face-to-face course to work within the online environment, and revising an existing online course.

Chapter Five, Using Workload Strategies for Maintaining Quality of Life, expands on the four major types of workload strategies (design, support, teaching, and time allocation) that resulted from the study findings covered in Chapter One. We present the workload strategies as practical tips and guides for new and experienced online instructors, describing approaches to managing workload that correspond with each type. Our goal for this chapter is to focus on quality of life, an essential component of instructor well-being.

We end the book with Chapter Six, Final Thoughts and Practical Implications for Balancing Workload. In this chapter we remind readers about the benefits and limitations of the changing educational landscape, and about the potential opportunities for instructors. We also provide recommendations on how instructors can take advantage of and embrace these opportunities. Further, we suggest a four-step rethinking process for prioritizing time and managing workload. We conclude our book by identifying practical implications for balancing workload.

SUGGESTIONS FOR READING THIS BOOK

The way we have organized the book provides readers with different options for selecting what is most relevant to them. We recommend that those new to the field of distance education read through the chapters in a linear fashion. The first chapter sets the stage for the rest of the book, and we encourage everyone to read this chapter. The second chapter provides 14 instructors' stories, which we summarize in a table. This table can help readers select the most relevant stories to meet their needs. The following three chapters focus on practical examples and implications for instructor workload when teaching online. For those who are seasoned in the field, these final chapters will help them reflect on and expand their practice. We also include a glossary of terms to assist readers in understanding new terminology.

ACKNOWLEDGMENTS

This is the second book that we have coauthored in the *Jossey-Bass Guides to Online Teaching and Learning* series. The process we use in our writing is exceptionally enjoyable and rewarding, as we bring together our research and practical experiences; reflect on the information we have gathered; and discuss, deliberate, and arrive at a consensus that is both stimulating and gratifying. The insights and strategies that have evolved during the writing of this book have already helped us reflect on new ideas and implement these in our own online teaching practices.

We are most grateful to all of the study participants who completed the online survey and particularly to those who gave their time to reflect on and describe their workload strategies through in-depth interviews. Their insights have made this book a valuable resource for other instructors, instructional designers, practitioners, and administrators. We are also indebted to the Consulting Office for Research and Evaluation (CORE) at the University of Wisconsin-Milwaukee School of Education for its transcription services, under the coordination of Ling-Lun (Crystal) Chien. Our editors, Erin Null and Alison Knowles, provided us with outstanding support and encouragement from start to finish. Their rapid responses to our e-mails and requests helped our writing move along smoothly.

It is increasingly apparent to us that we would not be able to maintain our quality of life without the support of all of our caring family members. Rosemary's husband, Don Lehman, was our *get to work* support, who reminded us that we need to be disciplined but also flexible—and have fun. Thanks as well to Simone's sister, Aline, and mother, Gladis, who provided loving support through Skype and during Simone's visits to Brazil while on her yearlong sabbatical. And we cannot forget that our book-writing sessions in Madison and Milwaukee also involved the presence of our affectionate and mischievous cats—Ceb, Maggie, and Peaches. Their company during our writing process kept us grounded as we stopped, took breaks from our continuous writing, and gave them our full attention. Family support is an integral part of the strategies we use to manage our workload when writing and teaching online. It provides the foundation for maintaining our quality of life.

Simone C. O. Conceição   Rosemary M. Lehman
Milwaukee, Wisconsin   Madison, Wisconsin

ABOUT THE AUTHORS

Simone C. O. Conceição, PhD, is an associate professor of adult and continuing education and teaches courses in the areas of distance education, the use of technology with adult learners, instructional design, and principles and foundations of adult learning. She received her doctorate in adult and distance education from the University of Wisconsin-Madison, and her master's in adult and continuing leadership education from the University of Wisconsin-Milwaukee. Her dissertation focused on faculty experiences teaching online. This book is an extension of that research.

She coauthored the book *147 Practical Tips for Teaching Online Groups: Essentials for Web-Based Education* (2000) and is the editor of *Teaching Strategies in the Online Environment* (2007). Most recently, she coauthored the book *Creating a Sense of Presence in Online Teaching: How to "Be There" for Distance Learners* (2010).

Dr. Conceição's research interests include adult learning, distance education, the impact of technology on teaching and learning, instructional design, learning objects, and staff development and training. She was born in Brazil, and has lived in the United States since 1989. Her diverse background brings an international perspective to the fields of education and training. She has researched and identified many aspects of good practice in online environments, and is an expert in helping instructors and trainers understand Web-based technology tools, software, and design processes. She received the 2006 Early Career Award from the Commission of Professors of Adult Education.

Rosemary M. Lehman, PhD, is an author and consultant in the field of distance education and a partner in eInterface. She has 20 years experience working for the University of Wisconsin-Extension as a senior outreach and distance education specialist, and as the manager of the Instructional Communications Systems Learning Design and Outreach Team. In these positions, she taught online and supervised faculty, staff, government, and nonprofit personnel in selecting, designing for, and effectively using distance education technologies. She received her doctorate in distance education and adult learning, and her master's in television and media critique, from the University of Wisconsin-Madison.

She authored *The Essential Videoconferencing Guide: 7 Keys to Success* (2001), edited *Using Distance Education Technology: Effective Practices* (2002), coauthored *147 Practical Tips for Synchronous and Blended Technology Teaching and Learning* (2007), and coauthored *Creating a Sense of Presence in Online Teaching: How to "Be There" for Distance Learners* (2010).

Dr. Lehman's research interests and areas of expertise include instructional design; synchronous and blended technologies; perception, emotion, and cognition at a distance; educational applications for media and technology; the development and integration of learning objects; and technology accessibility. She has led numerous workshops on distance education; has served as a keynote speaker and presented at statewide, national, and international conferences; and was the recipient of the 2005 University of Wisconsin-Extension Award for Excellence in distance education and leadership.

Managing Online
Instructor Workload

Issues and Challenges When Teaching Online

I think online education has opened up opportunities that some of our learners wouldn't have had. . . . It has allowed them so much flexibility.

Ellen

Online learning in higher education is growing at a rapid pace, and online learners have surpassed the total higher education learner population. In fall 2007, over 3.9 million learners were enrolled in at least one online course in the United States. This was a 12% increase over the number from the previous year (Allen & Seaman, 2008). This growth in market demands can provide both benefits and limitations for the fields of online and higher education.

Some of the benefits of rapid growth are the greater impact on the economy, the increased geographical reach of institutions across states and countries, better access for nontraditional learners to educational opportunities, more convenience and flexibility for learners and instructors, new opportunities for interactive and collaborative experiences, and increased knowledge and skills relevant to the use of technology on the part of all participants (Allen & Seaman, 2008; Conceição, 2006; Thompson, 2004).

Some of the limitations are that educational organizations are increasingly offering online courses as "cash cows," top-down demands are escalating the responsibilities of instructors unprepared to teach online, instructors' perceptions are leading them to believe that online teaching takes more time and effort than face-to-face instruction, some view online education as a "second-class" learning experience, and teaching online has lower credibility for tenure and promotion (Allen & Seaman, 2008; Maguire, 2005; Mupinga & Maughan, 2008; Wilson, 1998).

Due to the market demands, a large number of institutions of higher education are now providing online programs, pressuring instructors to move their existing traditional courses to the online environment or create new online courses. As a result, it is necessary for instructors to take a fresh look at their teaching, adapt their course design, modify their teaching strategies, and rethink how they prioritize and manage their workload.

Effective online teaching calls for intentional design and creating a sense of presence and connection between instructor and learners. Creating a sense of presence involves an awareness and understanding of how to "be there" for the online learner (Lehman & Conceição, 2010). Designing, delivering, and evaluating online instruction, in comparison to face-to-face instruction, require a distinctive type of management, which depends on the components of the design process (such as content type, course format, strategies, instructor role, technology, and support) and factors that influence workload (such as number of courses taught, learner enrollment, position held, and instructor responsibilities).

Managing the online teaching workload has become a concern for both new and experienced instructors. This concern is frequently the result of demands from the administration; a perception that the online environment is omnipresent and operates 24 hours a day, 7 days a week; a lack of understanding of the elements that make up the distance learning environment; inexperience in designing online instruction; and a lack of awareness of the importance of being present with learners online. With the increasing growth of online offerings and institutional pressures, instructors are at a loss and feel overwhelmed by not understanding how to deal with workload.

Until now it has been difficult for instructors to find the information and assistance they need to address workload management when teaching online, because most of the information found in publications is based on opinions, reviews, and anecdotes (Bower, 2001; Carnevale, 2004; DiSalvio, 2007; Dunlap, 2005; Dykman & Davis, 2008; Lorenzetti, 2007; Scheuermann, 2005; Sheridan, 2006), and a small number of empirical studies (Andersen & Avery, 2008; Betts, 1998; DiBiase, 2004; Thompson, 2004; Wilson, 1998; Zuckweiler, Schniederjans, & Ball, 2004). Therefore, this book will address institutional and instructional issues and challenges of workload management in higher education, stories from instructors in different teaching positions on how they balance their workload, the reality of managing workload when teaching online from a design perspective, the different ways instructors can manage tasks and prioritize time for online courses, and workload strategies for maintaining quality of life.

INSTITUTIONAL ISSUES AND CHALLENGES

When we refer to institutional issues, we mean important questions, situations, or events that need to be resolved and can affect online instructor workload. These institutional issues are static, and through awareness they become visible and capable of being moved forward through action. Institutional issues present challenges that higher education organizations deal with when considering the new online teaching and learning environment. These challenges can be acted upon to resolve the institutional issues. Table 1.1 addresses four of the institutional issues and challenges most common to online teaching in higher education.

Market Demands

Institutions of higher education must embrace the idea that online teaching is a reality they must act upon if they want to compete in the world economy. With the decrease in financial support, public institutions are suffering and in need of new markets. For many institutions, public or private, online education has become a new form of revenue that does not require them to build additional physical facilities, and that has proven to be a solid source of income with increasing enrollments (Allen & Seaman, 2008; Maguire, 2005). In addition to bringing in revenue, online education provides better access, convenience, and flexibility for adult learners who would not otherwise be able to further their education, and it has become a major focus for higher education institutions (Miller & Husmann, 1999). This calls for a shift in the institutional paradigm (O'Quinn & Corry, 2002).

Table 1.1

Institutional Issues and Challenges in Online Teaching

Issue	Challenge
1. How do market demands affect online instructor workload?	1. An increased online learner population requires systems thinking for instructor empowerment, support, incentives, and rewards in order to offer efficient and effective online education.
2. How does the institutional perspective affect online instructor workload?	2. Online education requires innovative institutional perspectives to determine appropriate online instructor workload in the changing higher education landscape.
3. How do the institutional definition and recognition of workload affect the online instructor?	3. Institutions must determine equitable workload policies and procedures for online teaching.
4. How does program quality affect online instructor workload?	4. Institutions must provide online instructor support for developing quality online programs that show meaningful outcomes based on competencies through assessments.

The new institutional paradigm requires systems thinking, the process of understanding and guiding change in a higher education institution. This change spans from simple to complex and involves all parts of the organization as they influence one another within a whole. When traditional higher education institutions consider including online education in their offerings, they must integrate it into their institutional system. The same type of services that are provided for traditional face-to-face programs should be adapted for the online environment. For example, student services, technology support, and instructor support are some of the provisions that should be carefully examined and developed before offering the online program.

Systems thinking addresses how this paradigm shift affects both the role of the instructor and instructor workload. O'Quinn and Corry (2002, p. 1) describe this impact on instructor workload by stating that not only does online education demand that instructors "learn how to use new technologies, it also requires a paradigm shift in how educators orchestrate the act of learning." The starting point of this paradigm shift is the intrinsic motivation and openness to change on the part of the instructor—and a feeling of empowerment. The institution must be aware of what is needed to appeal to instructors who are new to online education. Instructors are more likely to be motivated to change paradigms if they are provided with extrinsic motivators, including instructor support, incentives, and rewards (Maguire, 2005).

An institution can provide instructor support that is administrative, monetary, and technical. Administrative support involves policy changes that will enable instructors to gain promotion and tenure as a result of teaching online. Monetary support, in the form of stipends, professional development, overload pay, merit pay, or increased salary, is also an incentive for instructors to be motivated to teach online. Institutional rewards include release time, recognition, and technology acquisition (Maguire, 2005).

As a result of an increased online learner population and market demands for higher education institutions, the challenge is how to shift from a traditional paradigm to systems thinking, while taking into consideration how these demands affect instructors and their workload. Another challenge is to motivate instructors through empowerment, support, incentives, and rewards in order to offer efficient and effective online education.

Institutional Perspective on Instructor Workload

The old brick-and-mortar concept of higher education is being transformed. In the old mode, learners live on campus, walk to classes, attend regular courses during normal working hours, participate in campus activities, and socialize with other learners within the confines of the campus area. This mode still exists; however, the landscape is changing. Even though learners still live within the university boundaries, they are adapting their campus lifestyle to the changing times. Today the use of mobile technology has revolutionized the way learners live, communicate, and interact. Campus living now offers easy access to networks and wireless technology. Learners are no longer tied to physical locations for communicating, instead carrying mobile devices. Interactions happen anywhere, anytime, any pace through social networking sites.

A typical first-year learner in the United States today lives in a dorm; has a laptop; carries a cell phone or handheld device; is constantly interacting with friends, other learners, and family members through texting or social networking sites; and participates in a mix of face-to-face, hybrid, and online courses. Some of the campus behaviors in the traditional mode remain; however, emerging technologies have added another dimension for learning, communicating, and interacting. Carroll-Barefield, Smith, Prince, and Campbell (2005) call this change the "brick and click": learners enjoy traditional campus living with the advantages of the innovative use of technology, creating a new landscape for higher education.

In this new landscape, instructors must also adapt to keep pace with the changes. An instructor's role is less that of a lecturer and more that of a facilitator. Often learners expect that the instructor is available all the time, that course materials will be accessible in the learning management system ahead of course time, that the instructor will immediately respond to e-mail messages, and that the course materials will be delivered in a variety of technology formats. These expectations are challenges for instructors as well as administrators when addressing issues of workload.

For instructors, because of these expectations, the concept of workload is being redefined. Learner demand for Web-based, hybrid, or online courses is altering the way instruction is delivered. To keep up with this challenge, instructors must be open to change, have technology skills, become familiar with the online environment, and consider innovative ways to meet learners' needs. For administrators, the issue is how institutional perspectives can address instructor workload.

The challenge is how to deal with these expectations and view teaching and learning from a new perspective that involves reexamining the concept of workload. Should workload be based on credit hours, class size, or lab work? Should workload be measured differently for various disciplines? Should course preparation time be included in the workload? Should the workload be distinctive when teaching undergraduate versus graduate classes? These are some of the many questions administrators must address.

Institutional Definition and Recognition of Workload

There are varying definitions of workload in the literature. Definitions often account for time and task and depend on a variety of factors that influence each other. From an institutional viewpoint, these factors include the type of institution (public or private, two-year or four-year, technical or community); policies and procedures that guide institutional practices (number of courses taught, learner enrollment, level of instruction [undergraduate or graduate], type of class [Web-based, hybrid, or online]); the instructor's position ranking within an institution (faculty member, teaching academic staff member, part-time or adjunct instructor); infrastructure support (technology acquisition, technical assistance, professional development); and instructor union affiliation.

Institutions of higher education tend to account for workload using metric systems that vary from classroom credit hours to weighted teaching units. Classroom credit hours are learner-instructor classroom contact hours. Weighted teaching units are equivalent to the amount of workload credit an instructor earns for teaching (Ehrlich, 2003). Research-based institutions divide the workload among teaching, research, and service obligations. Other institutions, such as community colleges, technical schools, and two-year colleges, place more value on the teaching and service responsibilities of the academic workload and less or none on research.

The metric systems used by higher education institutions may be a good fit for brick-and-mortar settings in which, for example, an instructor who is teaching a three-credit undergraduate lecture course has contact with learners for three 50-minute periods per week. When the same class is taught online, however, contact hours become difficult to determine; and time spent in an online class per week does not adequately represent instructional responsibilities (Mupinga & Maughan, 2008).

A recurring theme in the online education literature is that online teaching demands more work and effort than traditional face-to-face teaching (Conceição, 2006; DiBiase & Rademacher, 2005; DiSalvio, 2007; Euben, 2003). Yet there are different ways of looking at this. One way is to consider the level of instructor experience. Inexperienced instructors are more likely to spend more time and be less efficient when they first start teaching online. Another way is to compare the design components and strategies instructors use. Most frequently, online instructors' perception of having more work than they would with face-to-face teaching stems from their inability to prioritize and manage workload. Thus the issue is how institutional definition and recognition of workload affect the online instructor. The challenge for institutions is to foster equitable workload practices through their policies and procedures.

Program Quality and Instructor Workload

From an institutional standpoint, program quality is essential in order to stay competitive in our uncertain economic times. Due to this uncertainty, institutions are converting many traditional programs to the online environment or are creating new ones. But the conversion or development of a new program is not a simple task; it requires time, effort, and innovation. It involves determining the appropriate conversion or new program procedures, revising or developing program competencies, creating a plan for designing or redesigning the course, developing online course materials, and implementing the curriculum (Carroll-Barefield, Smith, Prince, & Campbell, 2005). Although these tasks appear to be strictly administrative, they require instructor involvement and additional workload responsibilities, particularly at the planning and implementation phases. This extra involvement and work can increase instructor workload, but also help ensure program quality.

Some of the reasons for instructors' being involved in the process of converting a program for online education include their connection to the existing program, the necessity of curriculum adjustments, the need for instructors to establish a sense of presence, and the institution's use of a systems approach to transition the program to the new environment. Instructor involvement is key. The institution should provide instructors with administrative, monetary, and technical assistance as the starting point for embarking on this online venture.

As for designing new programs, instructor involvement begins with curriculum development at the departmental level. It then continues with the creation of the online education system (including such components as registration, design, learner support, and so on) and with forging connections with other units in the institution.

Once the converted or new programs are ready to launch, measures to control for program quality should be in place. To achieve quality control, all involved (from administrators to instructors) should be part of the evaluation process. Ongoing assessment strategies might include preprogram surveys, midprogram evaluations, seeking continuous learner feedback, postprogram surveys, and alumni impact evaluation (conducted one or two years following learners' completion of the program).

INSTRUCTIONAL ISSUES AND CHALLENGES

When we refer to instructional issues, we refer to instructional questions, situations, or events relating to institutional infrastructure, design, time allocation, and successful teaching that can affect instructor workload. These instructional issues are always present, although we may not be aware of them. Through awareness, these issues become visible. Instructional issues present challenges that can be resolved through the use of institutional policies or instructional strategies. Table 1.2 shows four examples of instructional issues and challenges related to online teaching workload in higher education.

Table 1.2
Instructional Issues and Challenges in Online Teaching

Issue	Challenge
1. What kind of institutional infrastructure do online instructors need to function in the online environment?	1. Effective online instruction requires institutional support and reasonable policies concerning instructor workload.
2. What makes the online environment different, and how can instructors understand this difference?	2. Online teaching is different from face-to-face teaching and requires a new way of thinking for designing and delivering instruction. Instructors must be able to make the online environment feel real by creating a sense of presence through strategies, while at the same time being mindful of workload.
3. How can instructors allocate their time effectively when teaching online?	3. Teaching online demands organization, task management, and prioritization to effectively balance the workload.
4. How do instructors manage online teaching, balance their workload, and maintain quality of life?	4. With a sound institutional infrastructure, effective design approaches, efficient time allocation, and useful strategies, instructors can successfully balance their workload.

Institutional Infrastructure

There are many instructors who are intimidated by online teaching, and studies of instructor workload have found a number of factors that limit instructor participation in online teaching. These factors can be grouped into five categories: lack of monetary support, lack of rewards, lack of infrastructure support, bias against teaching online, and concerns about quality (O'Quinn & Corry, 2002; Thompson, 2004; Zuckweiler, Schniederjans, & Ball, 2004).

Lack of monetary support is evident in an institution's reluctance to provide stipends, salary increases, merit pay, royalties for copyright materials, and reimbursement for expenses. Deficiencies in promotion and tenure, release time, recognition, and professional prestige indicate the lack of rewards. Weak infrastructure support is demonstrated by inadequate technology and technical assistance, clerical staff, and professional development training, and by minimal encouragement from departmental colleagues (O'Quinn & Corry, 2002).

For some instructors, teaching online is like having a new persona; they think they will lose control over their classroom, that they will have to teach in an uncomfortable setting, and that their instructor role will change considerably. In addition, they think that working in a collaborative team environment will be an unpleasant experience. Course quality and the quality of learners who are participating in the courses are also concerns of instructors who are reluctant to teach online (O'Quinn & Corry, 2002).

In addition to the five categories of factors, for some instructors adding online teaching to their workload can be a threat because of the perceived time commitment to new tasks (such as communicating over e-mail, responding to discussion boards, keeping electronic office hours, and so on), which would increase their workload and reduce productivity for research. Instructors are also reluctant to teach online because of the time they think it will take them to develop and deliver online courses. Class size is one more factor that inhibits instructors from participating in the online environment. As class size increases, class management can expand instructor workload (Zuckweiler, Schniederjans, & Ball, 2004).

Some of the concerns that inhibit instructors from teaching online are based on misperceptions of and inexperience with the online environment. It is not a matter of more or less work to teach online; rather, it is different work (Moore, 2000). As mentioned before, workload depends on a variety of factors that influence each other. Concerns about workload tend to lessen over time as instructors become more familiar with the online environment, become more experienced, and work more efficiently. However, without a strong institutional infrastructure in place, these concerns are less likely to be resolved.

The issue is to have an institutional infrastructure that encompasses, for example, the administrative, monetary, and technical assistance instructors need to function in the online environment as well as reasonable policies on instructor workload. Depending on the institution (private or public), faculty governance, or union affiliations, the challenge is to create institutional policies that will specify the course of action for online instructor workload.

What Makes the Online Environment Different

When we enter new territory, we tend to use known approaches to accomplish tasks and familiarize ourselves with the new setting. It is human nature to use the same process when converting courses to the online environment. For example, instructors' first reaction is to take their existing course materials and transfer them to the Web-based environment. Simply transferring courses to the Web, however, is not the answer (Carroll-Barefield, Smith, Prince, & Campbell, 2005). This type of change requires a new frame of mind and way of thinking, feeling, and behaving. From an instructional standpoint, it involves planning, intention, and design in order to ensure effective learning outcomes and meet quality standards (Lehman & Conceição, 2010).

There is a decided difference between the face-to-face and online environments. In the face-to-face environment, we can clearly see our learners, hear their voices, and touch concrete objects within the walls of the classroom. Because of this closeness, we are able to use our senses to have eye contact, hear voice nuance, read body language, move around the room, and pick up objects to demonstrate course concepts. Conversely, the online environment is elusive. We are unable to see or hear our learners, unless we incorporate specific technologies. We have to think carefully about how we can relate to the learners, create a sense of closeness, and explicitly describe our actions.

For instructors to recognize these differences, they need to understand the "big picture" of online education. Imagine an online course as part of a subsystem (program) within a large system (university). The large system includes many components, such as registration, learner services, technical assistance, and instructional design support. The subsystem includes the curriculum, instructors, and learners. Then there is the online course, with a syllabus, readings, course materials, assessments, and so on. All of these elements are tangible.

We can see, hear, or touch them . . . but in the online environment they are virtual. For learners to feel the virtual as real, the instructor must create a sense of presence.

The concept of presence in the online environment is not easy to understand. It involves perceptual presence, "the sensory experience of 'being there' and 'being together' [with others] in the online environment. It involves the recognition of the online environment and actions in response to this environment. Through the perceptual process, which involves thought, emotion, and behavior, individuals interact with information and others and feel as though they are together in this learning experience" (Lehman & Conceição, 2010, p. 130).

Integrating presence in online courses is a gradual process. It begins with planning. For new and existing online courses, planning starts well ahead of the delivery of the course. Presence should be intentionally incorporated into the design process by identifying the types of experience and ways in which we experience presence through activities and interactions. Planning, intention, and design require time, energy, and creativity and can influence instructor workload; however, workload is contingent upon the discipline, the course format, interactive strategies, the instructor role, technologies, and support.

The issue for instructors is to understand what makes the online environment different. The challenge is to think in a new way when designing and delivering instruction by developing instructional strategies that make the online environment feel real through the creation of a sense of presence—while at the same time being mindful of their workload.

Allocation of Time for Online Design and Delivery

For online instructors, time for designing and delivering their courses is a major concern (Conceição, 2006; Dunlap, 2005; Wilson, 1998). This concern is related to the intense work that spans from the design to the delivery of the course. This length of engagement can even start before instruction, continue during the delivery of the course, and be complete when the course ends. This engagement requires depth during the delivery of the course; the process "involves the full use of one's ability, energy, or resources" (Conceição, 2006, p. 35).

If instructors are new to online teaching, this process may be even lengthier because they will need training in the use of technology and pedagogical approaches for online teaching. Time invested in the design of a course varies from situation to situation, but researchers nevertheless have tried to calculate the time spent on the design and delivery portions of a given online course. For example, Wilson (1998) reports a mean of 152 hours spent per course. Her study included 35 participants from the disciplines of social science, the humanities, scientific or technical studies, and business. Participants were from large and regional universities, community colleges or technical schools, and correspondence programs.

Andersen and Avery (2008) conducted a study of 11 Web-based graduate nursing courses to determine the time required to teach, and they compared that finding to the time necessary for teaching similar courses in the face-to-face environment. Their study did not include predesign time. Findings indicate that instructors spent an average of 46.1 hours per credit per course. Out of these hours, 12% were spent preparing during the semester, whereas 52% were spent interacting with learners. According to the results of this study, there was no significant difference in the teaching hours spent per credit in a Web-based course versus those spent in a face-to-face course.

Studies by Visser (2000) and DiBiase (2000), comparing face-to-face and online courses, were reported in the same issue of the *American Journal of Distance Education*. Their studies had some similarities, but different results. Visser says that nearly twice as much time is needed to teach online in comparison to face-to-face. DiBiase, on the other hand, says that less time is needed per hour per learner in the online class compared to a face-to-face course. It is important to note that the courses these researchers examined were very different in terms of content, learner characteristics, institutional support, and technology tools used.

Comparisons between face-to-face and online courses can be misleading and must be cautiously conducted. As a baseline, instructor experience and institutional infrastructure should be considered. There are different types of variables that have an impact on the dynamics of online courses and influence instructor workload: behavioral, cognitive, and affective. The behavioral variable is observable and can be acted upon, and includes certain types of tasks, interactions between the instructor and learners, course expectations, and the length and depth of engagement. For example, we can write a list of tasks to accomplish while teaching online. We can interact with learners through the discussion board. We can set course expectations by being explicit in the syllabus. We can track time spent and instances of engagement in the online environment.

The cognitive variable is the effort related to the thought process for delivering the course (Conceição, 2006). Components of this variable might include, for example, staying engaged with learners in a discussion board conversation on a specific topic; making a mental effort to keep the class focused; involving learners in team brainstorming; and creating an illusion of presence through realism (close match between the real and the virtual world), immersion (illusion through virtual reality), involvement (interactive engagement with the learner and others), and suspension of disbelief (psychological "letting go" of reality) (Conceição, 2006; Lehman & Conceição, 2010).

The affective variable is the effort related to feelings that result from emotional presence in the online environment due to the lack of physical presence (Conceição, 2006). Emotional presence is "the ability to genuinely show feelings through words, symbols, and interactions with others in the online environment. In this process, learners are emotionally present when they connect with others in an authentic way during the online learning experience" (Lehman & Conceição, 2010, p. 130).

How instructors deal with the behavioral, cognitive, and affective variables during the design and delivery of an online course will have an impact on their workload. Instructors tend to think and say that online teaching is work-intensive. Is this a perception or a reality? The issue is how instructors allocate their time effectively when teaching online. The challenge for them is to identify strategies that can help them organize their courses, manage tasks, and prioritize time.

Online Teaching and Quality of Life

Online education is now a part of the higher education landscape and cannot be overlooked. It has had an impact on institutions, learners, and instructors, and institutions of higher education have to think about innovative ways to offer programs. Online education has helped learners both gain more access to learning and enjoy the convenience and flexibility of anywhere, anytime, any pace instruction. For instructors, it has provided new opportunities to challenge their intellect, develop new ideas, learn about and use new technologies, and reach new audiences (Betts, 1998).

In spite of these positive attributes of online education, a significant number of instructors avoid online teaching. Many of the reasons for resisting participation include insufficient institutional support or incentives, having to change their teaching mind-set, intensive work for course design and delivery, large class size, learner characteristics, difficult working hours and a feeling as if they are on call all the time, and the time taken away from research productivity. These reasons are understandable and in any combination can affect instructors' quality of life.

According to Palloff and Pratt (2011), providing sufficient training and incentives is critical. Inadequate support and a lack of incentives mean that instructors will increase their workload and will not earn equitable compensation. Instructors' need to change their mind-set can result in disturbing their usual ways of doing things and adding new tasks to their workload. Unfamiliarity with the online environment can entail intensive work for course design and delivery, particularly in the early stages, and large-size online classes without adequate support can double instructors' workload by requiring them to maintain ongoing communication with learners. The level of learners in regard to their undergraduate or graduate status, background experience, special needs, and so on can also increase workload, as instructors seek to provide the extra support learners need during the delivery of the course.

Often instructors feel that it is difficult to establish a set time to check on the status of a course and communicate with learners. As a result, they think they are always on call and constantly monitoring, making it challenging to find any free time for their personal life. Further, instructors in research-based universities are more likely to avoid teaching online because it takes time away from their research. If they assume online teaching responsibilities, they are at risk of reducing their research productivity (Zuckweiler, Schniederjans, & Ball, 2004).

The issue at hand is how instructors manage online teaching, balance their workload, and maintain their quality of life. With a sound institutional infrastructure, effective design approaches, efficient allocation of time, and useful strategies, instructors can successfully balance their workload.

OUR STUDY ON INSTRUCTOR WORKLOAD WHEN TEACHING ONLINE

As a preparation for writing this book, we felt that we needed to gain insights from instructors who teach in the online environment. We decided to conduct a study to investigate what strategies instructors in institutions of higher education use to balance their workload when teaching online. Using purposeful sampling we asked instructors working at two- and four-year institutions—and who had taught at least one course totally online—to participate in our study. We sent out messages via instructor listservs and personal e-mail correspondence to instructors others had recommended. We then conducted an online survey of 38 participants and interviewed 14 instructors from a variety of roles and institutional settings. Our survey and interview protocols were based on our framework for designing instruction with a sense of presence, which we will discuss further in Chapter Three (Lehman & Conceição, 2010).

We looked at the survey responses and in-depth interviews to explore emerging themes related to strategies instructors use to balance their workload when teaching online. To ensure that the results of our study were trustworthy, we worked together to examine these themes and had extensive discussions of the findings through debriefing. In order to minimize the influence of our judgment over the study, we used a confirmability audit to verify the information with some of the participants we interviewed. We also peer-reviewed the interview transcripts to determine if the information supported our conclusions.

Our study findings provided us with practical insights from new and experienced instructors from the disciplines of education, health care, natural science, computer science, business, and the humanities. We asked survey participants to base their answers on one online course that they had taught. Out of 38 participants, 47% selected an undergraduate course, whereas 53% selected a graduate course. Courses varied in duration from 4 weeks (5%), 8 weeks (5%), 15 or 16 weeks (84%), and other (6%). Enrollment varied from 10 to 100 individuals in a course. Study participants' experiences teaching online ranged from teaching the course once (32%), twice (18%), three times (16%), to more than four times (34%). More comprehensive details about study findings can be found elsewhere (Conceição & Lehman, 2010).

Findings revealed four major types of strategies that instructors used to help balance workload when teaching online: design strategies, support strategies, teaching strategies, and time allocation strategies. *Design strategies* are tasks completed before the online course begins and during the delivery of the course. *Support strategies* are dependent on the instructor's level of experience in online teaching, the type of course taught, and learners' needs, and include one-on-one support, peer support, institutional support, and external support.

Teaching strategies encompass administrative, facilitative, and evaluative tasks carried out during the delivery of the course. *Time allocation strategies* are a major concern for instructors who teach online because they depend on the course discipline, the support received, course enrollment, and the technology used. To manage their time, instructors need to be organized, disciplined, able to distinguish between work and personal life, and yet flexible.

SUMMARY

Online learning in higher education is growing at a rapid pace and brings both benefits and limitations. The benefits have an impact on institutional growth, whereas the limitations affect instructional workload. With this growth, higher education institutions experience issues and challenges related to shifting market demands, the institutional perspective on instructor workload, institutional definition and recognition of workload, and program quality and instructor workload. At the same time that institutions benefit from this growth, they must consider and address the instructional issues and challenges associated with such expansion, which can have an impact on institutional infrastructure, differences in the online environment, time allocation for online design and delivery, and online teaching and quality of life.

In Chapter Two we will share instructor stories for balancing workload from some of the participants in our study, who work in different teaching positions. In Chapter Three we will explain how to distinguish among the types of necessary course tasks and how they can be accomplished within a design framework. In Chapter Four we will provide three examples of how to manage tasks and prioritize time for online courses. In Chapter Five we will address workload strategies in detail, based on our study findings and our own experience. We will end the book with final thoughts and practical implications for balancing workload.

Instructors' Stories for Balancing Workload

chapter
TWO

I block my schedule for teaching online. I close my office door. This way people know they should not socialize with me at this time. It's like . . . "Don't bother me, I'm teaching now."

Kay

In Chapter One we introduced you to the study we conducted in preparation for this book. In this chapter we expand on our findings and share comprehensive accounts from some of the study participants, concentrating on the approaches they use for balancing workload when teaching online. We use stories captured from 14 interviews with online instructors in higher education to illustrate these approaches, presenting each account in light of the instructor's background, strategies used to balance workload, and a summary of the story's major themes.

The 14 stories we selected represent a variety of disciplines, positions held, course durations, levels of instruction, and instructor experience. We use pseudonyms to identify the instructors in our stories and maintain confidentiality. Our aim is to focus on the strategies that most concern instructors who teach online. In some cases, these strategies overlap. It is our hope that instructors will be able to identify with some of these stories, learn from them, and apply them to their own practice. Table 2.1 is a summary of the 14 stories addressed in this chapter so that instructors can easily access information relevant to their needs.

CO-TEACHING AS A STRATEGY FOR BALANCING WORKLOAD

Lauri, an associate professor at a four-year institution, teaches three-credit online linguistics courses at the undergraduate and graduate levels. Her course load is the equivalent of 2.5 courses per semester. She teaches during the regular 15- or 16-week semester with an enrollment of 10 to 25 participants per course. Lauri's online courses are content-focused, and she co-teaches them with a colleague. In addition to teaching, she also has administrative duties as a coordinator of a certificate program. Lauri dedicates one day a week for her research. In order to balance her research and service responsibilities, she is not involved with teaching during the summer term. She uses design, support, teaching, and time allocation strategies to balance her workload.

Design Strategies

When creating her online courses, Lauri uses a number of design strategies to balance her workload. She spends 20 to 30 hours a week for one online course, versus 5 to 10 hours a week for a face-to-face course, and uses the following strategies to reduce her workload: having another instructor teach the online course with her, structuring the course in an organized way, reducing required readings, providing clear guidelines for discussions, and dividing learners into groups.

Having a co-instructor work with her in an online course can be a time-saver when they assign each other tasks during the design phase. By designing a well-organized online course that is easy to follow, instructors avoid numerous questions from their learners at the outset of the semester. This can considerably reduce their workload.

Another design strategy that has been effective for Lauri is reducing required readings per learner. To do this, she divides the learners into two groups and assigns specific readings for each group. Each group can go into more depth with the assigned readings, and then share what they have learned with the whole class. This way of dividing the readings reduces workload without missing any of

Table 2.1
Summary of Instructors' Stories for Balancing Workload

Discipline	Instruction Level	Enrollment	Position Ranking	Story Focus
Linguistics	Undergraduate/Graduate	10–25	Associate professor	Co-teaching
Adult education	Graduate	22	Assistant professor	Planning ahead
Psychology	Undergraduate	40–100	Associate professor	Giving individual feedback
Early childhood	Undergraduate Graduate	25–28	Teaching academic staff member	Time management
Health care	Undergraduate	12–20	Clinical assistant professor	Blocking out time
Sociology	Undergraduate	25–35	Professor	Teaching during short terms
Health care	Undergraduate	16–24	Community college instructor	Using time allocation strategies when teaching for multiple institutions
Science	Undergraduate	20	Community college assistant professor	Teaching from home
Education	Graduate	20	Associate professor	Years of experience
Sociology	Undergraduate	20	Adjunct professor	Teaching for several institutions
Health care	Graduate	15–33	Professor	Time-saving cohort program
Education	Undergraduate	26	Graduate assistant ad hoc instructor consultant	Managing tasks for multiple online courses
Education	Graduate	15	Instructional designer Instructor	Recurring mixed-mode online courses, co-teaching
International education	Undergraduate	20	Administrative academic staff member Instructor	Current information driving content

the content. An essential part of this design strategy is to develop clear guidelines for discussions when dividing learners into groups. Having learners form groups as a strategy for other aspects of the course, such as research projects and presentations, can also be an efficient way to save time.

Support Strategies

Lauri and her co-instructor also make use of support strategies before and during a given course, such as obtaining technical support through the institution's help desk during preparation stages, offering orientation activities as part of learner support in the beginning of the course, and sharing other learners' stories about their online experiences in previous courses.

Teaching Strategies

Lauri considers co-teaching to be a time-saving strategy for her heavy-content courses. In her language translation courses, in which learners can focus on different languages, dividing learners between instructors facilitates the teaching-learning process. Each instructor carries the teaching load for a specific language. Lauri accomplishes this by setting specific guidelines for each instructor's role. Also, she considers it very important to get to know the co-instructor well during the design phase. Some teaching strategies that she uses during course delivery are assigning group activities and giving rapid responses to learners via e-mail.

Time Allocation Strategies

Lauri and her co-instructor believe that it is essential to create instructor presence in their online courses. To do this in an efficient way, they have a light presence during the week by answering general questions in the discussion area, and a heavier presence at the end of the week when they wrap up the discussion. Another strategy they use is asking learners to summarize and lead discussions.

Lauri reduces her time on each online course by reading learners' work on two monitors, with one screen containing the source text and the other screen showing the target text to be graded. With this strategy, she avoids having to tab between files. Because her courses are content-intensive, she also sets up blocks of time for teaching during the week (three to four days per week) and tells her learners that she is not available on weekends. Because she uses this time allocation strategy, learners know what to expect from her.

Summary of Main Strategies

In Lauri's case, co-teaching seems to work as part of her design strategy for the type of online course she teaches. Setting up clear guidelines for co-teaching is essential for efficient and effective online course delivery. This strategy may not work for everyone, but it is an option. It is important that instructors check their institution's policies and procedures regarding co-teaching. The best strategies are the ones that fit with the individual instructor's teaching style and lifestyle.

Focusing on a course during the week and avoiding weekend teaching works well for Lauri as a way to distinguish between her work and personal life. Balancing between light and heavy instructor presence during the week is an efficient way to manage the teaching workload. Selecting one day a week to work on her research prevents distractions from other responsibilities and keeps her organized with her research tasks. Finally, leaving the summer term for service responsibilities and research helps Lauri balance her other academic responsibilities.

PLANNING AHEAD AS A WAY TO PREDICT WORKLOAD

Stan, an assistant professor at a four-year institution, teaches three-credit adult education courses online at the graduate level. His academic load involves teaching three courses per semester, conducting research, and participating in service activities. He teaches both face-to-face and online courses during the regular 15- or 16-week semester, and teaches online courses during the summer. His courses average an enrollment of about 22 nontraditional learners. From his experience with nontraditional learners, who often work full-time and also have family obligations, he knows that he must design his online courses with a variety of options. That means planning ahead to meet learners' needs. For his online courses, he uses design, teaching, and time allocation strategies to balance his workload based on his learner population.

Design Strategies

Planning ahead of time is a key aspect of Stan's online courses. Because he has taught these courses a number of times, he has been able to refine, enhance, and develop more efficient strategies. When he first designed his online courses, he spent more hours creating activities and assessments. With subsequent courses, he has been able to draw on his past experiences and trim back the amount of time spent redesigning them.

Stan puts himself in the role of the learner when designing his online courses. It is essential for him to know his learners, effectively organize his online courses, and manage his time commitments. Stan's graduate-level learners are very motivated and self-directed. As part of his design strategies, he offers an optional face-to-face course orientation. His online courses are organized based on units. He uses once-a-week synchronous chats, group discussions, and individual assignments, but chooses not to include group work because his nontraditional learners would have a difficult time coordinating team tasks. Because of his concern that an online course is "really never over" in regard to time commitment, Stan believes in planning ahead to manage his workload. Another design strategy he uses to help save time for his subsequent course offerings is to have a folder with new ideas and notes taken during the delivery of the course. These ideas and notes serve as guides for when he redesigns that course.

Teaching Strategies

Because he has self-directed, motivated learners, Stan is able to involve learners in their own learning through interactions with their peers, but this requires a lot of up-front work at the beginning of the course. Stan's work then tapers off as learners become more independent and his role changes from that of an expert to that of a guide. This means that his time commitment on the course is reduced as it progresses. One of the teaching strategies Stan uses for encouraging learner interaction is having them critique each other's work.

Time Allocation Strategies

For Stan, planning ahead also means knowing how many hours he spends on an online course. In his situation, he spends about 80 hours per semester teaching each online course—an average of 5 hours per week, including some weekend time. He blocks out time in the morning to check the course, respond to e-mails, and participate in the discussion with learners. He announces that he responds to e-mails within 24 hours, so that course participants know what to expect.

Summary of Main Strategies

Stan understands that online courses don't just naturally happen. They require preplanning, organization, and intentional design. Preplanning helps instructors manage their workload, so that their workload doesn't manage them during their course delivery. Organization assists instructors in determining a framework for their content and activities, thus helping them know what to expect during each course sequence. Intentional design serves as the means for instructors to maximize the efficiency, effectiveness, and appeal of online teaching in order to meet and anticipate their learners' needs.

GIVING INDIVIDUAL FEEDBACK AS A WORKLOAD MANAGEMENT STRATEGY

Beatrice, an associate professor at a four-year institution, teaches three-credit psychology courses online at the undergraduate level. Her academic load includes teaching two courses per semester (one course is supervision), conducting research (70% of her time), and participating in service activities. She teaches online during the regular semester for 14 weeks and during the summer term for 4 weeks. Her course enrollment during the regular semester varies from 40 to 100, and during the summer term from 20 to 40. Her online courses are content-focused, and her activities are based on the course textbook. Her focus for workload management is on providing quality individual feedback on assignments. For her courses, she uses design, support, teaching, and time allocation strategies to balance her workload based on class enrollment.

Design Strategies

Beatrice organizes the course based on the course textbook and employs the PowerPoint files and quiz bank that come with it. Her online activities include an individual assignment, group discussions, and quizzes. She works one to two weeks prior to the beginning of the online course to revise it. Because her online course is based on the textbook, design is only a small piece of her workload. However, she still needs to revise the syllabus, course timeline, quiz bank, and structure of the learning management system before again offering the online course.

Support Strategies

Beatrice's institution provided her with instructional design training to prepare for online teaching. She also receives support in the form of a teaching assistant when course enrollment is high. The teaching assistant helps her manage her online courses by participating in the discussions and providing the majority of the learner feedback.

Teaching Strategies

During the delivery of the course, Beatrice uses orientation activities as a way to reduce learners' questions about the course structure and assignments and other concerns during the course. The individual assignment requires each learner to raise a virtual child. As part of this assignment, learners have to answer questions based on course concepts and theories as the child gets older, does different things, and has distinctive problems. The purpose of this assignment is for learners to understand these concepts and theories and apply them to their child.

Once learners have completed the individual assignment, they share their results with their group in the discussion forum. When the online course has a large enrollment, Beatrice divides the learners into seven discussion groups. In the discussion forum, learners have to post a 300- to 400-word message with their results, and then post a 200- to 300-word message in response to someone else's posting. As part of Beatrice's teaching strategies and instructor presence, she provides individual feedback through comments in a Word document.

Another teaching strategy Beatrice uses is conducting quizzes. These quizzes are part of the quiz bank from the textbook, contain multiple-choice questions, and provide an opportunity for learner feedback through a quiz dispute box. The quiz dispute box is used when learners think that their answer to a quiz question is correct, but the quiz program scores it as a wrong answer. Learners then have the opportunity through a specific procedure to dispute the answer. In addition to providing individual feedback to learners, Beatrice creates instructor presence by making herself available to learners, rapidly responding to their e-mails and regularly posting course announcements and reminders.

Time Allocation Strategies

Because of the nature of her courses and their high enrollment, Beatrice focuses the majority of her time on individual feedback rather than on course design or group discussions. She takes two days to grade assignments (five hours each day per assignment) for a class of 40 learners. Although she checks the learning management system constantly throughout the week, including weekends, she lets the learners know when she is not available. To make grading more efficient, she uses a Word document template with predesigned comments for learner feedback on the individual assignment.

Beatrice considers online teaching an improvement for her work-life balance because it provides her with increased flexibility through the use of technology.

It gives her an opportunity to teach summer courses from anywhere, and it enables her to better manage her work and personal life.

Summary of Main Strategies

By using predesigned content and selecting a key teaching aspect of the online course, like Beatrice does with feedback, instructors can better manage their workload when they have a course with high enrollment. Beatrice provides quick responses over e-mail. This can be a challenge for instructors whose learners perceive that they are available 24/7. The solution is to use teaching strategies that create boundaries and communicate these boundaries to the learners. Another teaching strategy in this situation is to draft a response to the learner while it is still fresh in the instructor's mind, but hold back on sending the response right away. This avoids learners' perception that the instructor will always answer their e-mails immediately.

MANAGING TIME, RATHER THAN TIME MANAGING YOU

Chuck, a teaching academic staff member at a four-year institution, conducts early childhood online courses at the undergraduate and graduate levels. His teaching workload changes from semester to semester, and course duration lasts from 10 to 12 or 16 weeks. Course enrollment varies from 25 to 28 participants. In a given term, including summer, he teaches two face-to-face courses and one online course. As part of his workload assignment, he is also the program manager. For Chuck, a type A personality, teaching online is a 24/7 commitment. It is difficult for him to disconnect; however, he has developed support, teaching, and time allocation strategies to manage his workload.

Support Strategies

Chuck has over 10 years of experience in online education. His course design, except for updates and revisions, is fairly well set. Even though his online courses repeat from year to year, however, he needs time during the prior term to prepare for the subsequent offering. As part of his support strategies, Chuck uses an orientation with detailed information about the online course as an introduction to the online environment and as a means of creating a context for learner comfort. It is at this point in the course that learners begin to build skills, confidence, and community. He also uses the help desk for learner support when technical problems arise.

Teaching Strategies

Chuck is a strong advocate for encouraging interactions, developing online relationships, and building communities. To accomplish this, he seeks to develop online activities that require intense learner and instructor presence, facilitating thoughtful group discussions, audio-narrated PowerPoint presentations, audio announcements, and project presentations.

Time Allocation Strategies

For Chuck, time commitment to online teaching is a passion. He spends a lot of time during the delivery of his online course, dedicating 20 hours a week. He blocks out time daily to check the online course, usually doing this in the early morning or evening. He prefers to check on the course a little bit every day, rather than in large chunks of time. He works during the day on other things, and manages learners' expectations by telling them through explicit communication when he will respond. Chuck also travels often and communicates to his learners when he will not have access to the online course. The pace of his online course is such that there is a flurry of learner activity at the beginning of the week and a slower pace toward the end of the week.

Summary of Main Strategies

For online instructors, managing time rather than time managing them can be a challenge. This is especially true for those who enjoy being connected 24/7, like Chuck. But this can be a trap. To resolve this challenge, it is important for instructors to identify time allocation strategies that can help them better manage their time. Chuck has over time developed strategies that meet his needs and help create a course that builds community. He sets up blocks of time to be connected to his online course, uses the community-building approach to involve course participants in learning from and assisting each other, and has a good sense of the pace of his online course. So instructors must think about what they can do to avoid being constantly connected with their courses, how they can share course responsibilities with their learners, and how they can allocate their time more efficiently.

BLOCKING OUT TIME FOR THE ONLINE COURSE

Kay is a clinical assistant professor on a 12-month contract at a four-year institution. She teaches three- to four-credit undergraduate courses in the discipline of health care. Her courses are offered during the regular 15- or 16-week semester and during the 12-week summer term. Her online course enrollment varies from 20 participants during the regular semester to 12 participants during the summer term. Being a clinical assistant professor, her responsibilities include teaching, administration, and service.

Kay's teaching workload involves 12 units per term: 7 to 10 credits of teaching, 1 credit for service, 1 to 3 credits for administration, and 0.5 credits for e-learning for the department. She teaches two online courses during the summer term. As part of her administrative duties, she coordinates a program within her discipline. Her face-to-face courses are hands-on and interactive. When moving her courses to the online environment, Kay had to rethink her workload by incorporating design, support, teaching, and time allocation strategies.

Design Strategies

Kay teaches two online courses per term, one face-to-face course, and one independent study. Her design strategies focus on how to distribute course activities to balance her workload among all courses at any given time. She spends 10 to 12 hours preparing the online courses before they start. Further, course design continues throughout the course duration, and she spends 4 hours per week designing the courses each term. During the summer, her online courses are high-intensity, but they are faster. Her main goal in the design phase of a given course is to develop a detailed syllabus about course expectations.

Support Strategies

Kay works in a field of practice that requires creativity, innovation, and enthusiasm. She is constantly seeking new resources for her courses when she attends conferences. She also involves learners in sharing resources as another support strategy. She is not a technology-savvy person, so she uses one-on-one support from the teaching and learning center at her institution, peer support, and institutional support through the help desk.

Teaching Strategies

Kay uses group discussions and incorporates games and creative activities as her teaching strategies. To manage her teaching workload, she communicates to learners her guidelines for responding to their e-mails (within 48 hours) and communicates her level of participation during the course delivery. To ensure she fulfills her communication obligations, she first checks the discussion forum and e-mails, and then moves on to other aspects of the online course.

Time Allocation Strategies

For Kay, being disciplined with the schedule for her online courses is a must. She reserves time in her calendar for teaching online. For example, Mondays and Wednesdays, she blocks out time from 9:00 a.m to noon for online courses by closing her office door and letting other colleagues know that she is teaching at that time. This means that she spends an average of six hours per week for each of her online courses. She monitors her courses every day as part of a mental checklist for the day. She schedules assignment due dates for Saturdays. Although she has set times to check her online courses, she also allows some flexibility in case personal issues arise, at which point she rearranges her schedule.

Summary of Main Strategies

For online instructors whose workload focuses primarily on teaching and service, blocking out time for online courses is critical for helping them manage their workload. Kay goes beyond blocking out time; she closes her office door to avoid distractions and dedicates exclusive time for her learners. When online instructors who are expected to work a regular 40-hour-per-week job do this, they indicate to their colleagues that they are allocating specific times for their online courses during regular work hours. Kay is very disciplined with implementing her closed-door approach, and also with checking her online courses every day as a way to mentally cross off her daily tasks.

TEACHING ONLINE DURING SHORT TERMS

Bruno is a full professor at a four-year institution who teaches courses in the discipline of sociology at the undergraduate level. His three-credit 100-level online courses are offered during the winter break (for three weeks) and summer term (for six weeks). Course enrollment varies from 25 to 35 participants. He teaches his online courses in these time periods as a way to focus specifically on his teaching and research—during these times he does not have any service responsibilities and is able to spend set hours for course and research activities. He uses design, support, teaching, and time allocation strategies to balance his workload.

Design Strategies

Bruno teaches two different online courses, one in each term. These courses are similar in focus, but vary slightly in methods to engage learners in the course content, depending on the duration of the course. The first time he designed his online courses, he spent about 40 hours to prepare the materials. Once having designed the courses, however, his time to prepare them for each offering was considerably reduced.

Support Strategies

Bruno started his adventure as an online instructor by seeking one-on-one instructional design support from the teaching and learning center at his institution. He discovered that he could obtain content ideas and course materials from external resources, such as a local center related to the course topics, short videos from YouTube, and historical society photos.

Teaching Strategies

Bruno uses a variety of teaching strategies for his online courses, incorporating PowerPoint lectures, short videos, group discussions, quizzes, papers, and interviews, and using the learning management system drop box to give learners personal feedback. The difference between the two online course offerings is the amount of content each course offering covers. For the shorter session, he removes some of the readings.

Time Allocation Strategies

To balance his workload, Bruno uses automated grading on quizzes, and group discussion grading instead of individual grading. He takes one weekend during his online teaching to catch up on grading and quiz preparation. Further, he provides grading online all the time, which is in contrast to the intense grading he undertakes periodically for face-to-face courses. During the summer he spends 20 hours per week for his online course and allocates 10 to 15 hours per week for his research activities.

Summary of Main Strategies

For instructors whose responsibilities involve teaching, research, and service, teaching online during shorter rather than longer academic terms, like Bruno does, can be an effective strategy for balancing workload. Service activities, such as attending committee meetings, participating at conferences, and completing institutional projects, can be time-consuming and sidetrack instructors from teaching and research. Online teaching and research activities require focus, discipline, committed blocks of time, and anticipation of course responsibilities. By choosing to teach online during short terms, instructors are able to dedicate focused time to their research, collecting fieldwork data from anywhere. Bruno found out early on which design, support, teaching, and time allocation strategies would both match this approach and help him balance his workload while also meeting his research obligations.

USING TIME ALLOCATION STRATEGIES WHEN TEACHING FOR MULTIPLE INSTITUTIONS

Ellen teaches online courses for more than one institution. Her primary responsibility is as an instructor for a community college, where she teaches online courses in health care at the undergraduate level. In her primary instructor position at the community college, union rules determine her duties. Her workload includes teaching an average of 17 credit hours per semester. If she teaches a three-credit online course, she gets a 5.8% workload attached to the online course. For example, a three-credit course would be the equivalent of 20% workload plus the added percentage for online courses. Each course must carry a minimum enrollment of 16 and a maximum of 24 participants. As part of her workload, she coordinates fieldwork with 20 learners, which accounts for 5% of her time. In addition, she is required to participate in service activities, a responsibility she meets as a member of three college committees that meet sporadically throughout the year.

Ellen also teaches online courses as an ad hoc instructor for two other institutions. These ad hoc positions focus primarily on teaching. For instructors one drawback of teaching at different institutions is not knowing if the institutions will use the same learning management system. In Ellen's case, each institution uses a different learning management system, which is a challenge in itself. As a veteran online instructor, she is able to manage her workload with minimal support strategies; however, she uses design, teaching, and time allocation strategies to function efficiently and effectively as an online instructor.

Design Strategies

When designing her online courses for each institution, Ellen considers planning ahead a necessity in order to manage her workload. In this planning she decides on all the course activities and assignments, including when they should be released in the learning management system. This provides her with full course control and the flexibility to change anything at the last minute during the delivery of the course. After she spends about 12 hours designing each course, her instructor tasks become a matter of administrative, facilitative, and evaluative functions.

Teaching Strategies

Ellen uses quizzes, group discussions, and projects. As part of the community college guidelines, she must return e-mails within 24 to 48 hours. When she teaches online for other institutions using different learning management systems, she considers teaching from home an effective strategy because she is not interrupted and can dedicate long periods of time for different courses.

Time Allocation Strategies

For the different online courses she teaches with a variety of learning management systems, Ellen blocks out small chunks of time early in the morning and during evening hours, except on the days she teaches on campus. She spends about seven hours on her online courses per week. Another strategy she uses is setting online office hours instead of campus office hours for the different courses, because online learners prefer corresponding electronically instead of going to campus to meet with her. Moreover, she teaches for different institutions, and it would be too difficult to hold office hours in widespread locations. In addition, setting up online office hours helps her avoid time commuting to campus and other transportation issues such as road construction and parking.

Summary of Main Strategies

Ellen's major challenges when teaching for a variety of institutions are allocating her time and keeping up with the different learning management systems. She has discovered that planning ahead by allocating time for her online courses, prioritizing course activities, setting up the release dates of course features in the learning management systems, and determining online office hours help her better manage her workload. This preplanning approach is a time-saver for instructors because it relieves them from having to be constantly monitoring the different features of the various learning management systems during course delivery. For example, when teaching multiple courses, it is difficult to remember the specific units and activities for each course. By presetting these, instructors free up time to participate in group discussions, provide learner feedback, and respond to participants' concerns.

TEACHING ONLINE EXCLUSIVELY FROM HOME

Brenda is an assistant professor, teaching for a community college with a focus on undergraduate instruction. Because of her community college affiliation, she has no research requirements and few service commitments. Brenda travels periodically to the community college campus for faculty meetings, but teaches online exclusively from home. Her discipline is science, and her courses' duration varies from 8 weeks to a full 15- or 16-week semester. Enrollment averages 20 learners per course. Her courses are primarily content-based. Brenda teaches six online 4-credit courses each semester, for a total of 24 credits. Two of these courses are beyond her regular workload. In addition, she mentors new online instructors two to three hours a week. Brenda has had past experience teaching online, through which she has developed specific design, support, teaching, and time allocation strategies.

Design Strategies

Planning and organization are central in the development of Brenda's courses. By completing most of this planning and organization ahead of time, Brenda is able to concentrate the majority of her teaching effort on monitoring learners' participation and responding to their needs. For any new course she develops, she spends about 100 hours. For a course that is already developed, she spends about 20 hours before it begins to update and revise her materials. Once the online course has begun, she spends another 2 hours per week to revise and update the course as it progresses. She is very meticulous with her course design and offers a variety of opportunities for learner interaction and engagement.

Support Strategies

When Brenda moved her courses from face-to-face to online, she received in-depth course design assistance from her institution to develop her curriculum units. Brenda also had the support of her institution's instructional designer for copyright clearance, Americans with Disabilities Act (ADA) compliance, and feedback on her courses. She now provides this valuable support to other new online instructors in the form of a mentorship.

Teaching Strategies

Brenda bases her online courses on carefully selected textbooks, and she uses an asynchronous discussion board with prompts along with lecture concept maps in which she highlights important parts of the assigned textbook readings for the learners. She also incorporates quizzes and an extensive webliography of Web links for additional resources. Central to her courses are two types of labs—a virtual "kitchen" lab in which materials can be gathered at home and a "wet" lab that requires a more traditional lab kit. By involving her learners in these lab experiences, she lessens the need for creating a heavy sense of presence. Rather, her learners, through engagement, create a sense of presence with each other while she is able to serve more as a guide.

Brenda's course participants are also involved in two large field projects during the semester, further engaging them in focused learning in which Brenda can guide and mentor them. Other activities she prepares prior to the beginning of each course are quizzes, a midterm, and a final exam. She then integrates these into the online course and keeps track of them using an online gradebook. Brenda's teaching strategies help her manage her workload and encourage learner motivation and self-directed opportunities.

Time Allocation Strategies

One of the most difficult areas for Brenda to control is boundary setting. Although teaching from home is very beneficial for her with her growing family, Brenda realized early on that she would have to set boundaries to prevent her online teaching from taking over her personal life. For this reason, she has allocated about 1.5 hours a day, seven days a week for working on the online courses. She is available 16 hours a day to respond asynchronously to learner questions and needs, and works her time around her family's schedule. For example, her children's nap time is a dedicated time during the day that she can use to focus on her online courses.

Brenda is careful to let her learners know when she will be unavailable. She occasionally uses synchronous technology for feedback, but only when requested. Another challenge for Brenda is her perception of her colleagues' skepticism of online instruction and her feelings of guilt. She believes that her colleagues do not value her time spent on online education, when actually she dedicates an extensive amount of time from preparation to delivery.

Summary of Main Strategies

Teaching online exclusively from home has its benefits, but it can also easily take over one's personal life. Brenda quickly realized that she needed to set boundaries in order to distinguish between her work life and her personal life. Although she is constantly connected to her online courses, she makes an effort to communicate to her learners the times when she is not accessible. Telling learners she is unavailable is a way for her to establish course expectations and have a sense of control over her personal life. In addition, Brenda perceives that her time spent on online teaching can be misleading to skeptical classroom instructors. However, online instructors do not need to feel a sense of guilt and prove the extent of their workload to others. Instead, they should focus on how to manage their workload to fit their needs and anticipate the needs of their learners. Everything else is irrelevant.

MANAGING WORKLOAD BASED ON YEARS OF EXPERIENCE

Simon is an associate professor in the field of education at a four-year institution; he teaches three graduate-level online courses per term. He is also the coordinator for his graduate program. His three-credit courses are offered during the 16-week semester, and also in the summer. They are all content-based. Each of his courses averages 20 enrolled participants. Simon has taught online for over 10 years, and he has been able to apply his extensive experience to his online courses. In addition to his teaching, Simon's other responsibilities include administration, research, and service. He uses design, teaching, and time allocation strategies to manage his workload based on his years of experience.

Design Strategies

Simon has discovered some essential workload management approaches in the area of design, drawing from his years of experience in online teaching and looking at the courses of others for new ideas and time-saving strategies. For example, some of his strategies are undertaking precourse preparation and organization, using various technologies, and soliciting learner feedback.

Simon's main design strategy is to prepare and organize content and activities prior to the start of his online courses. When Simon begins this preparation, he does so with his learners in mind. Placing himself in the role of the learner helps him better select his content and activities—and decide on the pace of his courses. It also assists him in deciding which technologies he will integrate into his online courses. He uses podcasts and YouTube videos, technology tools with which his learners are familiar and that readily engage them in the online courses.

Simon prepares the technology-based activities prior to offering the course, saving valuable time during the course delivery that he can instead use to create a sense of personal presence. Simon is also open to the ideas of his learners for course enhancement and improvement. Following the completion of each online course, he uses these ideas and his own reflections to help him revise subsequent courses. He is adamant about his learners having an online learning experience that is equal to or of higher quality than one in a face-to-face classroom.

Teaching Strategies

Simon uses various teaching strategies to balance his workload: creating a detailed syllabus, rapidly responding to e-mails, communicating to learners about his availability, using grading software, and making weekly announcements on audio and video.

Simon's syllabus includes all aspects of his online course in addition to his regular office hours. He is also dedicated to swiftly replying to course participants' e-mails, rather than letting them accumulate. He lets his learners know when he may be away at a conference or unavailable for other reasons. He also uses a grading software program on his notebook computer to write electronic comments on learners' papers rather than typing them. This software allows Simon to use the pen that comes with the notebook to write comments directly to the screen without typing them. He posts weekly announcements on audio podcasts and videos on YouTube. These announcements engage his learners, help them stay on task, and also give them the sense of ongoing instructor presence.

Time Allocation Strategies

With his online course preparation and materials organization accomplished well ahead of time, Simon is able to limit his online teaching time allocation to 10 to 15 hours a week per online course. By designating specific times for electronic office hours, he has created boundaries and is able to avoid unplanned interruptions from his learners.

Summary of Main Strategies

Instructors' experience can be a deciding factor in whether they are able to choose effective workload strategies, as is evident in Simon's case. For Simon, his own experience and that of others have served as valuable resources. As a result, he has become proficient in planning ahead of time, selecting appropriate technology-based activities, establishing detailed course materials, and reflecting on and revising course strategies. As new instructors learn through experience, they should be open to the ideas of their peers and also their learners.

TEACHING ONLINE FOR A VARIETY OF INSTITUTIONS

Angelo is an adjunct professor for three online universities, as well as a full-time public school counselor for children with special needs. He teaches content-focused courses in sociology at the undergraduate level, including three online nine-week courses per term year-round and one face-to-face course—all outside of his regular full-time job. His course enrollment averages 20 nontraditional learners with a wide age range. To balance his workload, he uses support, teaching, and time allocation strategies.

Support Strategies

Preparation for Angelo's first online course involved redesigning his face-to-face course for the online environment. This was accomplished in an intensive training program for instructors followed by a two-week internship at one of the online institutions, during which Angelo spent 25 hours per week for eight weeks to develop his online course. In the training program he learned about the institution and the learning management system. He had, however, little assistance in transitioning his face-to-face course to the online format, or in the integration of activities and teaching strategies. This was something he struggled with on his own.

Although this training program was lengthy and time-consuming, it served as a guide for his subsequent online course design. With this initial design preparation, he only needed to reset each successive course. Further, for each course he makes a special point of using a notebook to keep track of what he does and reflects on how he can use that in future courses. This approach helps him manage his multiple online courses and his personal life. Angelo's example illustrates how important it is to consider instructional design for transitioning courses from face-to-face to online, assistance that can help instructors minimize the time they spend on course design.

Teaching Strategies

As a part-time instructor for multiple online institutions, Angelo tends to teach similar courses on a regular basis. He has found that teaching an online course more than one time is a huge time-saver for him. To prevent confusion from working with learners from multiple courses and institutions, Angelo has developed an online form to get to know, monitor, and respond to learners during his online courses. He prints this information off and keeps it in a notebook for each course, so that he can easily identify individual learners, respond to them, or comment on their writing.

Angelo sets aside for himself blocks of focused time for writing and responding to his learners. He works very hard to lock in these time frames. For example, when he gets home from his day job, he takes a little break, and then dives in and tries to get quite a bit of work done before dinner. This is when he is most alert and can focus on his online teaching. For him, this is the time when he is most productive. He also has learned to save responses from learner feedback and reuse them for future courses.

Time Allocation Strategies

When online instructors first experience designing, developing, and teaching an online course, the time spent can be overwhelming. In Angelo's case, preplanning time for him, including his training, was about 250 hours. However, time spent for subsequent online courses was cut back significantly to about 15 hours for each course per week, which can represent overload for someone who has another full-time position. His rationale for working on overload is that he plans eventually to give up his full-time job and teach exclusively online.

Summary of Main Strategies

Teaching online for multiple institutions in addition to holding down a full-time job can be a challenge for at least three reasons: lengthy preparation time, constant learner monitoring, and the difficulty of allocating time for teaching. Angelo realizes that working hard on online course preparation, although time-consuming, can be a time-saver later, because once he has created a course design model he can reset his online courses more efficiently. He also recognizes that it can be difficult to monitor learners from different institutions during a given semester. He resolves this issue by using a form to easily identify his virtual learners and keep track of their progress. Finally, by blocking his time during hours when he is most productive, he is able to work more efficiently.

COHORT PROGRAM AS A TIME-SAVER

Rhianna is a health care professor and also holds an administrative position at a research-based four-year institution. She teaches regular semester cohort courses at the doctoral level, both online and face-to-face. She offers her online course every other year to meet the cohort requirement. Enrollment ranges from 15 to 33 participants. As a full professor with an administrative role, Rhianna is also involved in service activities and does a fair amount of traveling. Her online course for the cohort program is process-based. She uses design, support, teaching, and time allocation strategies to help balance her workload.

Design Strategies

According to Rhianna, once her course is designed there is a minimum of preparation. For that reason, she spends time prior to the online course making certain that it is well organized. Part of the instructional design for the cohort program is to have a consistent look and feel for the learners when they access the online courses. Although there is a consistent design framework for the cohort program, however, instructors are free to design their own courses, integrating what is most appropriate for the content they teach.

For Rhianna, first laying out the content according to modules helps her break information into topic areas. She then develops PowerPoint files with voice-overs, creates questions for the discussion forums, identifies appropriate assignments that capture the content, and determines the course pace. As she progresses with her teaching, she reflects on what her learners are accomplishing and refines the course. It is very important to Rhianna that her course participants have access to the online course material prior to the beginning of the semester. To accomplish this she communicates to her learners that the entire online course is available ahead of time, so that learners can plan ahead and be better prepared for the semester.

Support Strategies

Technology support provided for Rhianna in setting up her online course has been a time-saver. Her program allocates money for instructional design support for the creation of PowerPoint files with voice-overs, and for the integration of course materials in the learning management system. Once these time-consuming course materials are developed, they can be reused from semester to semester, saving time the instructor can spend on other academic responsibilities. Having support staff to assist in uploading materials to the learning management system can also minimize the time an instructor spends on an online course.

Teaching Strategies

Because Rhianna's courses are cohort-based, there is no need for an orientation for each one. In a cohort program, an orientation is provided at the beginning, when learners get to know each other and become familiar with the learning management system and the institutional support that is available. It is during this orientation time that learners become familiar with the program standards.

A time-saver for Rhianna in her cohort-based online course is to divide her learners into groups of five or six participants. Each participant posts comments individually and interacts with her and others in the discussion forum. When Rhianna participates in the discussions, she avoids answering immediately; rather, she reflects on her response and waits to post it until the next day. She believes that by doing this she serves more as a guide than as an expert for the learners, and allows them to analyze the course topic before she intervenes.

Another teaching strategy Rhianna uses is to foster cooperative work, whereby learners collaborate in groups but develop individual research questions, participate in discussions to learn from each other, and determine how they will implement their individual study. Part of this assignment is to write a complete research proposal that might actually be used in the future. Rhianna believes that relevance enhances learner engagement and participation.

Rhianna is very cognizant of the importance of creating a sense of presence for her learners. One of the ways she accomplishes this is through PowerPoint presentations with voice-overs. Another way is by communicating with her learners about when she is available and what her expectations are for them.

Time Allocation Strategies

Rhianna considers how to allocate time for her online course during the initial design phase. When she begins designing her course, she carefully blocks out times in her calendar for her work on the course during the semester. Although she plans her online course well, she is aware that there is a heavier time commitment earlier in the program, and that her time commitment becomes lighter as the cohort group begins to take on more responsibilities.

Rhianna realizes that when there are more learners enrolled in her online course, there will be more time intensity on her part. Knowing this in advance helps her reallocate her time. She spends 8 to 10 hours per week on her online course. She has decided that what works best for her is checking her course daily, sometimes in the evening, but mostly in the morning. Because she values her personal time, she only accesses her online course once on the weekend. However, she is also very sensitive to her learners' comments and questions, and maintains flexibility in adjusting her schedule to meet her course participants' needs.

Summary of Main Strategies

Teaching online in a cohort program is a design approach that can be a time-saver. Instructors can follow a standard design established by the program, and yet can shape their online courses based on their personality. Cohort learners tend to get to know each other as a learning community from the beginning of the program through a general orientation. This prevents instructors from having to create an orientation for each online course and facilitates relationship and trust building early on. Further, because learners are part of a cohort, instructors can more accurately predict learner behavior and anticipate course activities, giving them a better sense of time allocation.

MANAGING SIMILAR TASKS WHEN DESIGNING FOR MULTIPLE COURSES

Natalie is an ad hoc instructor at a four-year institution. She also works as a graduate assistant for a public university and a consultant for a private university. These jobs are part-time while she is working on her doctoral studies in the field of education. She teaches a three-credit undergraduate-level online course with an enrollment of 26 participants during a six-week summer term. Natalie considers herself a multitasker because she works in three different positions, carrying out similar tasks in varying capacities. For her, responsibilities of each position must have their own focus, space, and time. Workload management for her is not just about the course she teaches; it is also about setting boundaries between her work and personal life. Natalie uses design and time allocation strategies to manage her workload and ensure quality of life.

Design Strategies

As part of Natalie's work in three different positions, she helps instructors design their online courses. This can be confusing. Even though the tasks are similar, she completes them in different locations, for different people, using two learning management systems, and following different institutional procedures. For Natalie, online course design in each of the three instances needs to be accomplished in its own online space, time, and physical location.

Natalie prefers to design her own online course entirely in the learning management system in advance, because this allows her to incorporate voice-overs, videos, authored video resources, and scripts. For this she requires sophisticated technology, intensive blocks of time, and focused attention. While working for other instructors, Natalie completes tasks in small chunks as requested. With her own course design, she needs more dedicated time to develop her whole online course.

Time Allocation Strategies

Because of her multiple positions, Natalie needs to separate her work tasks in one job from those in another. Her main goal is to complete these tasks in a timely fashion. Although she enjoys being connected all the time, one of the drawbacks is that it is easy to mix up work responsibilities with social connections. This is a challenge that Natalie seeks to overcome by scheduling specific times for her online coursework. She completes her most important tasks, like grading, when she is most alert, such as late mornings or early evenings. She usually provides feedback at the beginning of the week (on Monday evenings) for about 3 hours. She also creates a schedule for her learners outlining when to post responses to the discussions. For example, she might ask them to submit responses by Wednesday and Saturday every week. She spends an average of 10 hours a week on the online course. Her habit of being constantly connected makes her check her online course at least once in the morning and twice in the evening. She also has virtual office hours for learners to meet with her for questions or concerns about the online course.

Summary of Main Strategies

For online instructors who work in different positions doing similar tasks, like Natalie does, managing workload can be complicated. Because instructors in this situation must distinguish between the various tasks, to adequately accomplish them they need to allocate specific online space and physical space, as well as time. In an era when the Internet is ever-present from job to job and in our personal schedule, setting boundaries and holding to them make up the solution.

TEACHING A RECURRING MIXED-MODE ONLINE COURSE

Rosalina is an academic staff member for an outreach institution. Her experience with online education involves co-teaching a grant-funded course in the discipline of education. This one-credit graduate-level online course has an enrollment of 15 participants and is offered for six semesters on a recurring basis for a total of three years. This online course involves considerable preparation in the beginning because it is offered through a mixed-mode approach that incorporates synchronous videoconferencing and asynchronous online interactions. Rosalina's role in the outreach institution encompasses instructional design, teaching, training, and instructor support; and teaching counts for 15% of her time. Rosalina uses design, teaching, and time allocation strategies to manage her workload.

Design Strategies

Rosalina's first priority for designing the course is to put herself in the role of the learner. In this mixed-mode online course, design involves developing the syllabus and teaching units, gathering electronic resources, creating protocols for videoconferencing, making videos on DVD, practicing videoconferencing before the beginning of the course, and placing the course materials in the learning management system. The design phase is shared with two other instructional designers. One instructional designer helps with developing content and activities, while the other one incorporates these in the learning management system. For this online course, support is a part of the team approach. Each team member is assigned specific tasks and works in a collaborative manner.

Teaching Strategies

The mixed-mode course includes an orientation on videoconferencing and online activities. In this course, learners regularly participate in project-based activities (group and individual) and interact in the discussion forum. They also complete course evaluations on a continual basis, providing formative feedback on the online course that will help Rosalina and her co-instructors refine and reshape the course. Learners work independently, and the instructors serve as content experts, facilitators, and resources.

Time Allocation Strategies

For Rosalina, co-teaching is a way to manage her workload. Each instructor is responsible for specific duties related to the online course. When the course was first designed, the team spent about 10 hours a week for 12 weeks. Now that the course is developed, each time the course is subsequently offered it takes 5 hours of revision. One way the instructors manage the course workload is by having strict guidelines for the discussion forum, such as specifying the maximum number of meaningful posts per learner per week, limiting the number of words per post, and designating learner-shared leadership roles. Another strategy the instructors use is to take on the role of resource specialist, allowing learners to work more independently.

Summary of Main Strategies

Online courses that are offered on a recurring basis can provide time-saving benefits. In Rosalina's situation, the team was aware that the mixed-mode online course was going to be taught for the duration of the grant project, and therefore invested a sizeable amount of time in the design phase. They also knew that once the course design was completed, they would have to spend less time for revisions in future course offerings. The team approach is also a way to balance workload, because each team member can be assigned specific tasks before and during the course delivery. Finally, although courses that include synchronous and asynchronous technologies can be time-consuming for instructors, with the use of protocols and guidelines—and with sufficient practice—instructors can reduce their workload.

MANAGING WORKLOAD WHEN CURRENT INFORMATION DRIVES CONTENT

Sandy is an academic staff member for an international organization within a four-year higher education institution. Her primary position within this organization involves administrative work; however, she is responsible for teaching one four-credit undergraduate online course on international education. Sandy's online course has an average enrollment of 20 participants and is offered during the regular academic semester from 8 to 16 weeks in duration. The course content focuses on current global issues. This means that her course must be updated each time she teaches it. Sandy uses design, support, teaching, and time allocation strategies to manage her workload.

Design Strategies

Because Sandy's online course content requires up-to-date information, she bases the design of her course on the textbook and the most current news. The textbook provides a framework for identifying the global issues, which she then enriches with more current events occurring in the world at the time of the course delivery. Once she identifies the global issues, she incorporates them into modules in the learning management system, inviting speakers to create podcasts and supplying links to other podcasts and news events. She then creates the activities for each module, including discussion forum participation, team projects, and a mandatory orientation.

The need for timely content in her course necessitates advance planning and organization. The first time she designed the online course, Sandy started planning two months ahead of time. But once she designed the first online course, she used the template for that course as a model for subsequent offerings. Using the model she was able to reduce her time for course design and have the course ready to be released for the learners two weeks prior to the beginning of the semester.

Advance organization is essential when coordinating course speakers who are identified based on expertise in current issues. These speakers may participate either synchronously or asynchronously. For synchronous participation of invited guests, Sandy has to schedule time and equipment in advance. For asynchronous speaker participation, she has to prerecord and post the guest lecture in the learning management system before the course begins.

Support Strategies

Sandy uses the textbook, guest speakers, podcasts, and Web links as external support. She considers the textbook to be a dynamic resource tool, a springboard to identify and search for new content information. Guest speakers bring fresh perspectives to the current global topics. As mentioned earlier, in addition to creating podcasts of guest speakers, Sandy also incorporates podcasts from the Internet and Web links related to global issues into her course. She also seeks peer support, and models her online teaching on that of other colleagues who have used effective strategies, such as working to understand learner expectations and creating rubrics to grade assignments.

Teaching Strategies

Instructor presence is an important feature of Sandy's online course. Her instructor presence begins with the course orientation, during which she introduces herself to the group and invites learners to share personal information with each other. She makes the orientation a mandatory activity because she believes that participation will help learners be more comfortable online and feel a sense of community.

Although she uses one-way content presentation of global issues in her course, she also participates in interactive activities with her learners as a content expert, observer, and facilitator. As a content expert, she searches for current information that enhances the textbook. As an observer, she monitors the discussion forum from the sidelines and steps in when necessary. As a facilitator, she looks at learners' contributions and works with them to construct knowledge. Sandy also uses a team project to bring content together at the end of her online course.

Time Allocation Strategies

For Sandy, time allocation is a challenging task. Even though she only teaches one online course at a time along with meeting her administrative responsibilities, she struggles with setting boundaries. She has streamlined her time allocation for the design stage of her online course by preplanning and organizing her course materials, recycling existing resources, and using a dynamic textbook. However, Sandy is still overwhelmed with some aspects of the course delivery.

Sandy spends 15 to 20 hours each week updating the current news for the online course, checking on the discussion forum, and grading learner assignments. She is constantly checking her online course, but she does set boundaries for certain tasks. She blocks out time for grading on Monday morning and periodically checks the discussion board to avoid having to do intense work all at once. She also limits the number of discussion board postings per week as a way to reduce her workload. As she sees the need, she also checks the course on weekends, but she doesn't do this at a regularly scheduled time.

Summary of Main Strategies

Managing workload when the content must be kept current for the course can be a challenge. Sandy has discovered efficient strategies to reduce workload prior to the beginning of the course: she plans ahead, organizes course materials based on external resources, and prioritizes her time. Advance planning helps Sandy focus on the teaching rather than the design during the delivery of the course. In general, using a variety of external resources as a support strategy can enhance learner experience, reduce instructor workload during the delivery of the course, and provide flexibility when reusing the resources in future courses. Lastly, prioritizing time and setting boundaries can be a time-saver for instructors whose teaching is one piece of their work responsibility.

SUMMARY

In this chapter we presented, through instructors' stories, concrete examples of strategies for balancing workload that can fit a variety of settings and apply to different contexts. Instructors may identify with some of these stories, but should keep in mind that the hours spent per week on online courses were only estimates, rather than recorded times for each course. Although some of the instructors in these examples are efficiently prioritizing their time, others are still discovering new ways to effectively manage their workload.

In Chapter Three we will explain how to select types of course tasks for online teaching and how they can be carried out within a design framework. Designing online courses requires preplanning, organization, and intention—and an understanding of the online environment. By looking at workload from a design perspective, instructors can better manage and prioritize their time.

Looking at Workload from a Design Perspective

First I make sure my online course is well organized and there is a consistent look and feel for the learners. I lay out the content based on modules to break the information into specific topic areas. Then I develop activities for the appropriate assignments that capture the content and determine the course pace.

Rhianna

Think about an instructor who teaches a traditional course that has been scheduled to be offered totally online in the next six months. This instructor has taught this course for the last five years within the walls of the classroom, but has never taught online. Where does the instructor begin? First, the instructor has to think about how the course is taught in the classroom by reflecting on and answering the following questions: What type of content was the focus of the course? What format or formats were considered in this course? What interactive strategies were used to engage learners? What role did the instructor play? What tools were employed to enhance the course? Was any support required for this course?

Often instructors think that they can take their traditional classroom materials and plunge into the online environment. But this doesn't work. It requires an understanding of this new teaching and learning environment, planning, and intentional design. Now let's compare the traditional classroom with the online environment. There is a difference in space—in one instance the instructor is in the same space with the learners (a tangible location); in the other instance the instructor is in an elusive virtual space. There is a difference in time—in one instance the instructor is working with a clear sense of time in the classroom; in the other instance the instructor is working with flexible concepts of time in the virtual space. There is a difference in boundaries—in one instance the instructor is with the learners in one location; in the other instance the instructor is present with the learners without geographical limits. There is a difference in the way the instructor uses the senses—in one instance the instructor is in close proximity with the learners and able to see and hear them and touch objects; in the other instance the instructor needs to adapt these senses to relate to the learners and create a sense of closeness.

Now think about teaching. Let's compare teaching in the two environments. There is a difference in the level of interaction with learners—in the physical environment the instructor can easily involve learners in discussions and hands-on activities, whereas in the online environment these must be carefully developed and put into action. There is a difference in the level of course planning—for the face-to-face course the instructor can add and adapt teaching strategies at the last minute, whereas in the online environment these strategies must be intentionally planned and designed ahead of time. There is a difference in the cognitive and affective teaching effort—in the traditional classroom the instructor knows the amount of time needed to focus the mind and emotions for the teaching, whereas in the online environment the instructor may feel always connected.

Now that you've had time to reflect, you can better understand the differences between the traditional classroom and the online environment. These differences have design implications for instructor workload. To understand instructor workload, the first step is to become aware of the types of tasks that can be accomplished when teaching online. In this chapter, we will help instructors identify the types of course tasks required for teaching online and provide a design framework for helping instructors plan their online courses. We conclude the chapter by offering our Template for Managing Tasks and Prioritizing Time, which can be used during course design and delivery.

IDENTIFYING COURSE TASKS

Identifying course tasks will allow the instructor to plan, prioritize, and manage the workload. Looking at such tangible factors as the number of learners in the course, the type and focus of content, the course format, the interactive strategies, the instructor role, the type of technology used, and the kind of support provided, it is possible to determine the instructor workload based on time spent on the tasks to be accomplished before, during, and at the end of the course. We have grouped these tasks into four types: design, administrative, facilitative, and evaluative. The tasks we identify in this book are not all-inclusive. They are meant to get the reader thinking about what is needed throughout the design and delivery of an online course.

Design Tasks

Design tasks are mostly accomplished before the course begins, but the instructor may also complete portions of the design during the delivery of the course. These tasks are determined by the kind of course the instructor is designing: new, converted, or revised. They establish the role or roles of the instructor in the course and depend on the type and focus of content, the course format, interactive strategies, technology use, and the support provided. The nature of the instructor's workload depends on how these elements are orchestrated.

Administrative Tasks

Administrative tasks involve communication, management, and support. Communication happens when instructors send announcements or post information in non-content-related areas of the course. Management concerns matters of assigning groups or teams, dealing with the technology, and monitoring participation. Technical support pertains to instructors' provisioning of technology assistance or help for learners in overcoming difficulties, such as writing course assignments when English is learners' second language, when learners lack writing skills, or when learners have special needs. Instructor workload is determined by learners' experience, technology use, and enrollment.

Facilitative Tasks

When completing facilitative tasks, instructors interact with learners or encourage them to interact with each other. These tasks require extended instructor and learner engagement during the delivery of the course and involve cognitive and affective efforts (Conceição, 2006). Cognitive efforts are associated with tasks involving setting an agenda and starting a discussion, asking questions, soliciting comments, reading online posts, and sharing resources. Affective efforts include encouraging participation, providing personal insights, and guiding group or team activities. Although we describe these two kinds of efforts separately, they often occur together in the online environment. Instructor workload is contingent on the depth of engagement during the delivery of the online course.

Evaluative Tasks

Evaluative tasks are related to judging learners' work and receiving formative course feedback from them. Tasks linked to learner work involve providing individual, group, or team feedback and grading assignments. Instructors can use formative course feedback, which occurs midcourse, to further enhance the course design and, in turn, the learning experience. Instructor workload is determined by the evaluative approaches used and is dependent on enrollment, course strategies, the evaluation tool selected, and when and how the evaluation is scheduled. Table 3.1 provides a summary of the course sequence and types of tasks for an online course, along with task descriptions.

Now that we have described the most common tasks that influence instructor workload, for the remainder of this chapter we will explain the importance of using an instructional design process, present an instructional design framework, and discuss how this framework can be used to balance workload based on tasks.

WHY IT IS IMPORTANT TO USE AN INSTRUCTIONAL DESIGN PROCESS

An instructional design process provides a systematic approach for developing an online course. During this process the instructor can identify the multifaceted components of an online course and create a blueprint for the teaching and learning experience. This blueprint is a detailed plan for everything that will happen in the course and provides the "big picture." It can involve flow charts, scripts, storyboards, timelines, software programs, and so on to depict the features of the course. Table 3.2 describes different methods for creating a course blueprint.

The instructional design process begins with determining if a new course will be created, an existing face-to-face course will be converted to the online environment, or an online course the instructor has previously taught will be

Table 3.1
Summary of Course Sequence, Types of Tasks,
and Task Descriptions

Course Sequence	Type of Task	Task Description
Before	Design	• Set up, convert, or revise course content (syllabus and course readings) • Establish or revise the timeline for course activities • Create, convert, or revise the course format • Create, convert, or revise course strategies • Develop or update technology-based materials • Develop or revise support materials (orientation) • Set up course features in the learning management system (LMS) or copy features from a previously taught course • Upload new or existing materials to the LMS • Activate the course • Send a welcome letter to learners before the course begins
During and at the end of the course	Administrative	• Communicate with learners through announcements • Assign learners to groups or teams in the LMS • Manage technology • Check learner participation and course interactions • Provide technical and instructional support
	Facilitative	• Set an agenda and start discussions in group forums • Ask questions during discussions, encourage participation, and solicit comments • Read learner posts and provide insights • Guide group or team activities • Share resources and solicit comments
	Evaluative	• Give individual and group or team feedback • Grade assignments • Receive midcourse feedback

Table 3.2
Methods for Creating a Course Blueprint

Flow Charts	The instructor can use flow charts to align course objectives, strategies, and assessments or organize the navigation elements in the learning management system.
Scripts	The instructor can use scripts when designing units to provide a conversational and personal tone, and for video and regular announcements.
Storyboards	Storyboards, which contain visualization, sequencing, and transitions, are useful for illustrating how the course will unfold and can depict a series of subunits within a unit.
Timelines	Timelines are sequences of events outlining the course as a whole. They can be helpful during the design process because they work as checklists for what needs to be accomplished.
Software Programs	Instructors can use software programs as templates for designing a course. There are programs available that allow instructors to reflect on the elements of the course and insert course details into the software.

revised. Once the instructor has decided on the starting point, the instructor should select a model or framework for developing the course. In the next section we suggest a framework for designing an online course with strategies to manage and balance the workload. Such a framework can assist the instructor in identifying the multiple components of an online course, planning and designing prior to course delivery, and managing the instructional process to ensure the desired learning outcomes.

DESIGN FRAMEWORK FOR CREATING A SENSE OF PRESENCE

In our book *Creating a Sense of Presence in Online Teaching: How to "Be There" for Distance Learners* (Lehman & Conceição, 2010), we introduced a framework for designing online courses with a sense of presence. The concept of presence relates to what makes an online course seem "real." For us, being present is "being there" and "being together" with others in teaching and learning in a virtual space. Figure 3.1 shows our framework for creating online courses with

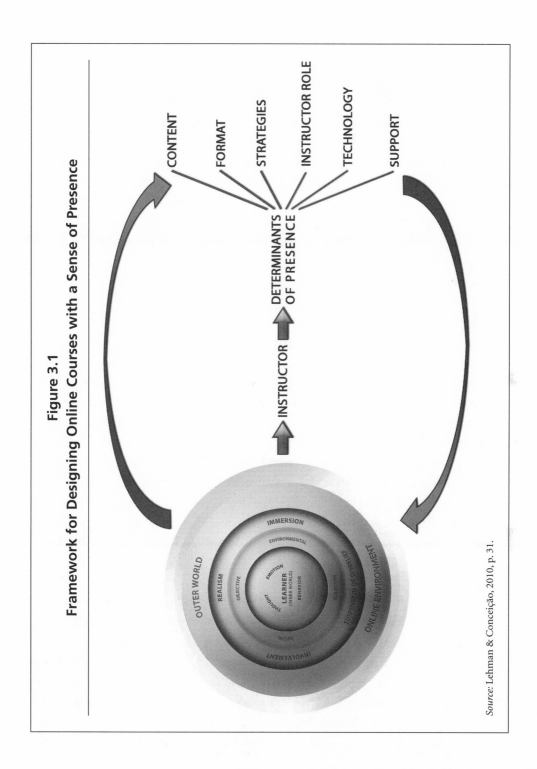

Figure 3.1

Framework for Designing Online Courses with a Sense of Presence

Source: Lehman & Conceição, 2010, p. 31.

a sense of presence, which provides the tools to understand the concept of presence and incorporates the elements necessary for designing online courses.

Within the framework, notice the Being There for the Online Learner model on the left. This model is a foundation for becoming aware of and understanding presence in an online environment. From the model to the instructor, there is a small arrow that corresponds to the instructor's awareness of how presence happens online. Following is a small arrow that goes from the instructor to the determinants of presence, denoting the path the instructor takes to design a course with a sense of presence. The determinants of presence—the components of the design process—direct the instructor to create presence in the online environment. The arrows arching above and below show the ongoing action inherent in using and revisiting the components of the framework. We will now address the elements of the framework in more detail.

Being There for the Online Learner Model

This model is characterized by a learner-centered approach. This means that an instructor views the learner as the center of the teaching and learning experience. The model comprises the inner and outer worlds of the learner, which interface with each other. The inner world of the learner consists of the dimensions of thought, emotion, and behavior in dynamic interplay. This dynamic interplay takes place in the online environment.

To design an online course with a sense of presence, it is important to consider four types of experience (subjective, objective, social, and environmental) that affect learning based on the course content and modes of presence (realism, immersion, involvement, and suspension of disbelief). Learners experience a sense of presence when they think, feel, and behave through interactions. The outcome is "being there" and "being together" for the online learning experience.

This model is circular in shape to represent a cylinder in motion containing three cylinders within it. At the center is the cylinder that represents the learner and the learner's perceptual process, which includes the dynamic interplay between thought, emotion, and behavior. The dark shaded lines between the learner and the types of experience and between the modes of presence and the online environment cylinders represent the interface between the inner and outer worlds of the learner. The two inner cylinders, the types of experience and the modes of presence, blend into each other and can occur in combination. The outside cylinder is the physical world of the learner connecting to the online environment via technology.

Determinants of Presence

In the framework, the determinants of presence are the type and focus of content, the learning experience format, the interactive strategies, the instructor role or roles, the technology or technologies employed in the course, and the types of support the instructor provides. These components can work interdependently, and based on how they are combined they can affect instructor workload. We will now discuss each of these design components and the implications for workload.

Content   The component of content is determined by the type of course— whether process-based or content-based. *Process-based courses* may include team or group work with tasks spread out over the delivery. In this case, instructor workload may be more intense in the beginning of the course, but can diminish as learners become more independent in completing course tasks.

Content-based courses may have a steady flow of discussions on topics throughout, and instructor workload can vary depending on the course objectives and depth of the discussions. If learners are active participants and take on leadership roles during the discussions, instructor workload can decrease. In this instance, however, if there are inexperienced learners, the instructor may need to provide more instructional support and model online discussions in the beginning of the course, moving to the background and becoming more of an observer or catalyst as the course progresses. Furthermore, instructors may choose to use a mix of both approaches and will need to balance workload between the two.

Format   Online courses may be self-paced, group-based, or a mix of both formats. In *self-paced courses,* the flow of the course reflects a more independent approach, with learners working at their own pace and time, communicating with the instructor at scheduled times or on an as-needed basis. In this format, learners' background and needs can dictate instructor workload. When working with learners who require special support, instructors will find that their workload can vary unpredictably throughout the course period.

In *group-based courses,* the instructor can serve as a facilitator of the group process and challenge learners to work collaboratively through discussions, projects, and fieldwork. In this format, the way the groups are structured and how well the learners interact and work with each other affect instructor workload.

If there are conflicts during group formation, the need for instructor intervention can add to the workload. With a mixed format, instructor workload depends on how the course is designed. By intentionally planning for individual and group learning experiences—and interspersing periods of high and low intensity—the instructor can have control and better manage the workload.

Strategies   Strategies engage learners with the instructor, the content, and each other, and can be instructor-led, logistical and instructional, cooperative, and collaborative. These strategies can have a decided effect on instructor workload based on the instructor role and intensity of tasks necessary to accomplish the strategies.

Instructor-led strategies are initiated by the instructor and involve tasks of communicating information (administrative task), assessing performance (evaluative task), monitoring learner progress (administrative task), and helping create a sense of presence (design task). Making instructor announcements; holding electronic office hours; offering support, mentoring, and tutoring; giving feedback on assignments; and uploading electronic portfolio feedback are some examples of instructor-led strategies. These strategies require planning and intentional design. Because of the lack of visual and auditory cues in the online environment, communication of information must be detailed and explicit, and performance assessment must be comprehensive.

On a regular basis during the beginning of the course, and less often as the course progresses, the instructor should monitor learner progress by reading their online posts or reviewing their learning management system progress reports. Instructor-led strategies can be time-intensive throughout the course, and workload depends on the instructor's management of the corresponding tasks.

Logistical and instructional strategies involve administrative or facilitative tasks. *Logistical strategies* facilitate interactions between instructor and learners in non-content-related discussion forums (Conceição & Schmidt, 2010). One task associated with these strategies is posting "housekeeping" messages related to logistical matters about the online course (administrative task). Having learners interact with other learners in non-content-related areas of the course to help each other can diminish instructor workload.

Instructional strategies involve one-way instructor content presentations to learners (design and facilitative tasks), such as mini-lectures, guest lectures, and object or picture demonstrations. The instructor must plan and design instructional strategies ahead of time because creating mini-lectures can be time-consuming when using technology. Also, inviting guest lecturers entails setting up the guest discussion and developing protocols in advance. And showing objects or pictures online involves the use of technology, and the instructor must consider copyright. These can all increase instructor workload during the pre-planning phase of the course, but reduce workload during course delivery.

Cooperative strategies pertain to interactions in which participants share, discuss, and synthesize ideas or concepts on a specific topic (facilitative tasks) through discussion forums, debates, or a fishbowl activity. In this last cooperative activity, learners are assigned to three separate groups: discussants, observers, and reporters. In their respective roles, each group brings an expanded perspective of a particular topic or issue. The instructor can take the role of a facilitator in the beginning of the course, eventually assign this responsibility to learners, and then become an observer and catalyst during the discussions. As learners become more independent and take on leadership roles in the discussions, instructor workload is diminished. Instructor participation in discussions can then focus on clarifying issues (administrative task) and challenging learners (facilitative task).

In an online course that includes *collaborative strategies,* learners can develop a team project or product that involves completing tasks and giving a final presentation. Examples of projects associated with collaborative strategies include case studies, digital storytelling, and virtual team assignments. The instructor role in this type of strategy can be one of an observer and evaluator who closely watches the group process and provides feedback throughout each part of the assignment (evaluative tasks). Providing periodic feedback to learners who are working collaboratively, instead of doing time-consuming, comprehensive grading at the end of the online course, can reduce instructor workload.

Instructor Role Instructors take different roles in the online environment depending on the tasks they accomplish before and during course delivery. If instructors develop a course from beginning to end and place it in the learning management system, they take on the role of *instructional designer.* In self-paced courses, in which learners work independently, the instructor can be a *tutor, mentor,* and *supporter.* For group-based courses, when using cooperative strategies, the instructor can take on the roles of *facilitator, catalyst,* and *evaluator.* For group-based courses, when using collaborative strategies, the instructor can act as an *observer, supporter,* and *evaluator.* In all cases, the instructor is also a learner by interacting with course participants and engaging in course activities.

Instructors must consider the types of activities they are planning for a course and determine the roles they will need to play. Their choices will affect their workload. For example, if a course has a mixed focus of both content and process and includes a combination of self-paced and group-based formats, instructors as course designers may want to intentionally sequence the course units in ways that will help them balance their workload. One way to do this is to select a few activities; run them throughout the course; determine the instructor roles; allot specific time for facilitation, observation, feedback, and evaluation; and fully communicate the process to learners. In doing so, instructors are in control of their roles, time, and tasks; learners know what to expect; and workload is therefore lessened.

Technology   The type of technology used in the online course can have an effect on instructor workload. Asynchronous (time delay) and synchronous (same time) technologies offer different experiences and are used for specific reasons. Although *asynchronous technologies* allow for flexibility with place, time, and pace, instructors may feel that they are always connected, giving the impression of an ever-present course. *Synchronous technologies* need to be scheduled at specific times and more closely resemble face-to-face interactive experiences.

Both asynchronous and synchronous online experiences require preplanning. The difference is with the types of tasks that instructors and learners need to accomplish, and when they must do so. On the one hand, for asynchronous learning, once an instructor has designed and uploaded the course to the learning management system, tasks involve facilitating, monitoring, and evaluating the activities. On the other hand, synchronous learning requires scheduling specific times for the interactions; arranging details; creating protocols; and facilitating and managing the activities (design, administrative, and facilitative tasks). Whereas using asynchronous technologies may give a feeling of always being connected to the course, synchronous technologies require more tasks up front—and the instructor knows the specific time frame for the activity.

Support   Learners in the online environment need instructional and technical support to function well. Although the instructor is the main connection for support, other support systems are available. *Instructional support* is the psychological and emotional assistance the instructor provides to learners throughout the course. This type of support is needed when learners indicate a lack of critical thinking skills or show signs of stress working in the online environment.

Learners receive *technical support* to help them overcome deficiencies in writing or in their understanding of technology. When an instructor supplies adequate support, learners become more at ease in the online environment, technology becomes more transparent, and distractions are minimized.

The instructor may be the first point of contact for support, but there are many strategies and resources that can help prevent extra instructor workload. For example, a well-designed orientation at the beginning of the course can direct learners to resources for assistance, avoiding potential problems early on. Also, by sending personal e-mails or holding electronic office hours, the instructor can help learners with psychological and emotional issues feel that they have support and encouragement to accomplish tasks, making them less likely to withdraw from the course. Group announcements can be an efficient form of communication to clarify concerns raised by multiple learners, and they can take up less time than working with learners individually. Finally, public forums can be effective vehicles for learner-to-learner technology troubleshooting, and they can reduce the need for instructor intervention.

Instructor feedback on learner performance during grading periods can be a good avenue of support. Feedback is individual, and the instructor can use this opportunity to direct the learners to resources, provide tips on how to solve problems, and give encouragement. The instructor can also point learners to such institutional facilities as the writing center or health care center. Other resources that might benefit learners include a Frequently Asked Questions (FAQ) Web site and support from learner groups, such as Lesbian, Gay, Bisexual, and Transgender (LGBT); multicultural; or women's resource centers. The instructor needs to provide links to these resources and strategies in the preplanning stages as a way to minimize or avoid potential problems learners may face.

If you are interested in a more comprehensive description of activities we have mentioned in this chapter, please refer to our book *Creating a Sense of Presence in Online Teaching: How to "Be There" for Distance Learners.*

USING A TEMPLATE TO MANAGE TASKS AND PRIORITIZE TIME

Once instructors become familiar with the design components that make online courses seem "real," they should understand that these elements are tangible factors that can be converted into tasks and time. Table 3.3 suggests a Template for

Table 3.3
Template for Managing Tasks and Prioritizing Time

Course Sequence	Type of Task	Week Number	Estimated Time Spent
Before	Design		
During and at the end of the course	Administrative		
	Facilitative		
	Evaluative		

Managing Tasks and Prioritizing Time that can serve as a guide for balancing workload when creating a new course, converting a face-to-face course to the online environment, or revising a course already taught online.

For new courses, the template can help instructors estimate the tasks and time spent during the design and delivery of the course. When converting a course, the template can assist in rethinking how to teach the course in the new environment. For existing online courses, the template can help instructors revisit their tasks and time spent and become more efficient when teaching the same course again.

SUMMARY

In this chapter we helped you recognize the types of course tasks required for teaching online. We also provided a design framework for identifying the multiple components of an online course. The framework can help an instructor plan and design an online course and manage the instructional process during the course delivery. We ended the chapter by offering a Template for Managing Tasks and Prioritizing Time, to be used when designing and delivering an online course.

In Chapter Four we will use the Template for Managing Tasks and Prioritizing Time to exemplify three ways to design and deliver an online course. These examples include the design of a new online course, conversion of a face-to-face course to the online environment, and revision of an existing online course.

Managing Tasks and Prioritizing Time

Planning and organization are central in the development of my online courses. Through this preplanning, I'm able to concentrate my teaching effort on monitoring learner participation and responding to their needs.

Brenda

I n Chapter Three we described the most common tasks that influence instructor workload, explained the importance of using an instructional design process, provided an instructional design framework, and offered a Template for Managing Tasks and Prioritizing Time for online courses. In this chapter we will use the template to describe three ways to design and deliver an online course based on its type, focusing on how to create a new online course, convert a face-to-face course to the online environment, and revise an existing online course. When addressing each type of course, we will first identify the course tangibles. Then, using the template, we will determine relevant course tasks based on the course sequence (before, during, and at the end of the course) and estimated time to complete them, and consider implications for instructor workload. Time estimates for designing and delivering an online course may depend on the course discipline, format, strategies, technology, instructor role, and support.

CREATING A NEW ONLINE COURSE

This first example presents a new online course in the discipline of chemistry, conducted by an assistant professor who teaches exclusively online at a private higher education institution.

Course Tangibles

This three-credit required undergraduate course has 20 learners from multiple disciplines. It is designed with a mixed content and lab focus, which includes both self-paced and group-based formats. The course involves group discussions, role-playing activities, virtual labs, "wet" and "kitchen" labs, and quizzes. Because this is a new online course, it requires many hours of preparation during its design portion. Teaching a new course, in addition to having a group of learners with different needs, can have a considerable impact on instructor workload.

The instructor has taught many face-to-face chemistry courses, but teaching chemistry courses online requires a new way of thinking. In this course the instructor plays many roles (designer, lecturer, facilitator, catalyst, mentor, tutor, observer, and supporter), and is always available for the learners via telephone, scheduled electronic office hours, or e-mail communication. In addition to having access to the course through the learning management system (LMS), learners read short lectures as text with embedded links; view video clips of the instructor explaining concepts (linked from an external site, such as YouTube); and have virtual chemistry lab experiences. An outsourced learning management system service provides orientation materials, reducing instructor preparation time. Table 4.1 summarizes the design elements for this new online course.

Course Sequence

There is no doubt that designing and delivering a new online course requires preplanning, time, and support. Creating a new online course is likely to take many hours and may require the following tasks: thinking in new ways, organizing materials in a format different from that used in the traditional classroom, designing strategies for the virtual environment, learning about the technology, bringing it all together, and creating the final product.

Table 4.1
Design Elements for a New Online Course

Content Type and Focus	Learning Format	Interactive Strategies	Instructor Roles	Types of Technology	Support
Survey	Self-paced	Discussion	Designer	LMS	Instructional
Chemistry	and	Role	Lecturer	PowerPoint	Technical
for Lab	group-	playing	Facilitator	with	
Science	based	Quizzes	Catalyst	voice-over	
Content-			Mentor	Internet-	
and			Tutor	supported	
lab-focused			Observer	virtual lab	
			Supporter	Video	

Before the Course Begins In this example, the instructor has taken 100 hours to design the new course, completing such design tasks as building the course structure, exploring course resources, selecting and evaluating lab activities, developing course units, and refining and finalizing the course. See Table 4.2 for detailed descriptions of tasks involved in the design phase.

Once a course is designed, instructor workload is reduced for the next time the instructor teaches the course. Institutional support for instructional design can help decrease the number of hours for developing the course. Professional instructional designers can guide instructors to envision the scope of the course as a whole and the sequence of units within the course. They can also assist instructors in designing graphics and PowerPoint materials, selecting interactive activities, using appropriate technologies, and creating instructor presence.

During and at the End of the Course For an instructor new to the online environment, administrative tasks can be time-consuming. The first time teaching a course, it is difficult to predict the amount of time the instructor will need to spend. In the online environment there is not a clear sense of time because of the flexible nature and elusiveness of virtual time and space. Checking learner participation and course interactions and responding to individual e-mails and phone calls from learners can result in a feeling of always being connected.

Table 4.2

Design Tasks for Building a New Online Course

Type of Design Task	Description	Hours Spent
Structuring the course	The instructor spends the first 5 hours building the "course home" structure, which contains the course syllabus, a virtual office, a Frequently Asked Questions (FAQ) discussion board, and links to such resources as the campus help desk, bookstore, and library.	5
Exploring course resources	Prior to actually developing course content, the instructor devotes time to exploring course resources, such as by reading the special topics and real-world applications sections within the chemistry textbook to make a mental list of possible discussion topics, and also searching for electronic images (molecular models and so on) that would not violate copyright laws and would visually enhance the course.	5
Selecting and evaluating lab activities	This design task involves searching for, evaluating, and selecting an appropriate laboratory kit for home use. Laboratory activities in online chemistry are divided between computer-based virtual labs; "kitchen" labs, whereby learners gather a few household items for testing; and "wet" chemistry activities requiring a more traditional laboratory kit.	12
Designing course units	This task involves designing eight content units (3.25 hours for each unit). Each unit contains learning outcomes, an asynchronous discussion board with prompts, a lecture and concept map that highlights important parts of assigned textbook readings, a quiz, Web links to additional resources, and a laboratory activity.	26
	Also, it takes additional time to develop units that contain a midterm exam and a final exam. It is important to note that online chemistry exams take longer to prepare than face-to-face exams if visual cues are embedded in the questions requiring essay responses. Multiple-choice and true-or-false questions are easier to program, but do not give the same range of data in regard to learners' progress toward learning outcomes.	12

	In addition to smaller laboratory activities included within each unit, the chemistry course contains two large field projects. These activities take approximately 10 hours each to develop.	20
	Compiling a webliography can take up to 5 hours. This involves surfing the Internet to select Web sites relevant to the course. The instructor includes a brief explanation next to the link to each Web site. This course contains approximately 30 webliography entries.	5
Refining the course	Having developed the course in its entirety, the instructor spends time tweaking the formatting of the "rough draft" course structure. This includes setting up the online gradebook; programming the course scheduler (which controls access to units, lists due dates, and so on); checking all margins in the learner view of the course; and making sure external links are active.	5
Finalizing the course	Finalizing the course includes writing course announcements, moving content around after reflecting on its initial placement, rereading and clarifying assorted descriptions and instructions, checking copyright and Americans with Disabilities Act (ADA) compliance with an on-campus instructional designer, and initiating a phone conversation with an instructional designer for an additional (optional) review of the course structure. This "finalizing" never really ends, even after 50-plus times of running the course.	10
TOTAL		100

New instructors need to carefully manage their time, so that time does not manage them.

The instructor may experience a sense of discomfort during communication and interactions with learners because of being unable to see or hear them without additional technology. An administrative task for a new course is managing the technology, and for someone who is new to the whole process of teaching online this can be overwhelming. In order to reduce technology anxiety on the part of instructors, institutional technical support should be in place.

New instructors may take on many roles during their first online course because of their inexperience and feelings of guilt. They tend to duplicate the same roles they play in the classroom when teaching online, but in the online environment these roles need a different focus because of the cognitive and affective efforts required. Also, instructors may perceive that other colleagues think they are not working as hard or as much because they are teaching online and not present in a tangible space. As a result, they may feel at fault and end up increasing their workload. But this should not be the case. The focus should be on balancing workload and meeting learners' needs.

In this first course example, the new instructor has taken on many roles and is available to learners between 10 a.m. and 7 p.m., seven days a week. This almost 24/7 availability affects instructor qualify of life. To correct this dilemma, instructors must schedule set times for communication with learners and inform learners of these expectations. Although it is important for instructors to be present for learners, it is equally important for them to prioritize, manage, and balance their work life and personal life.

In this course, the instructor uses lab activities, provides individual and group feedback, and grades assignments. Although developing quizzes can be work-intensive during the design portion of the course, such quick assessments can be time-savers for instructors during the course delivery, especially when the learning management system does some of the scoring. Giving individual feedback on lab assignments can be time-consuming when the course has high enrollment; conducting group grading can save time and lessen the instructor workload.

Undergraduate courses tend to require learners to complete a series of assignments. In a face-to-face environment, the instructor can easily collect these assignments in the classroom, give handwritten feedback, and return them during the following course session. Online, the instructor needs to download the assignments from the learning management system to a personal computer, review them and provide detailed electronic feedback, and then upload that feedback to the learning management system. These evaluative tasks are time-intensive at first. In this example, the instructor allows the option of "snail mailing" initial assignments the first few weeks of the course, particularly for adult learners who are feeling paralyzed by technology, because the intention is not to have the technology "become" the course for these learners. But as the course moves along and the instructor gets used to the process, using the technology becomes automatic and takes up less time.

As you may have noticed in this course example, the first online course has a greater instructor workload than subsequent offerings of the same course. As the instructor becomes more comfortable in the new environment, gains more experience, and discovers new ways to shape the online course, the workload decreases. Table 4.3 provides a summary of managing tasks and prioritizing time for a new online course.

Table 4.3
Managing Tasks and Prioritizing Time
for a New Online Course

Course Sequence	Type of Tasks	Time Period/ Frequency	Estimated Time Spent
Before the course	*Design Tasks* • Set up the syllabus and readings	• 2 months before the course begins	• 100 hours total
	• Establish a course timeline • Evaluate options for and set up the virtual lab environment • Create PowerPoint presentations with voice-overs • Upload materials to the LMS • Assign learners to teams • Activate the course in the LMS • Send a welcome letter	• 2 weeks before the course begins	

(continued)

Table 4.3
(continued)

Course Sequence	Type of Tasks	Time Period/ Frequency	Estimated Time Spent
During and at the end of the course	*Administrative Tasks* • Communicate with learners through announcements • Manage the technology • Check learner participation and course interactions • Provide technical and instructional support • Respond to individual e-mails and phone calls	• Daily as needed	• An average of 1.5 hours a day, including weekends (10.5 hours per week)
	Facilitative Tasks • Encourage participation and solicit comments • Read learners' online posts and provide insights • Guide lab activities	• Daily	
	Evaluative Tasks • Give individual and group feedback • Score quizzes • Grade assignments	• Biweekly	

CONVERTING A FACE-TO-FACE COURSE

Our second example describes the conversion to the online environment of a traditional face-to-face course in the discipline of health care.

Course Tangibles

This is a four-credit undergraduate course, offered for 12 weeks during the summer, with an enrollment of 20 participants. The instructor is new to the online environment and has minimal technology skills. Course participants are a mix of nontraditional and traditional learners with a range of technology skills, some requiring substantial technical support from the instructor. The course is part of a new online program.

This particular course is highly experiential in the face-to-face environment, involving group activities that facilitate interactions. The online course is a mix of self-paced and group-based formats. Self-paced projects include a scavenger hunt, open-book quizzes, and written assignments posted to the online drop box (such as self-assessing group leadership skills, watching a video and critiquing it, describing a program in two pages, and writing a three- to five-page reflection paper).

Group-based activities include a team project, group discussions in which learners share icebreakers and debriefing tools, and a discussion of a relevant case study. Learners are assigned to small groups of four or five individuals. Table 4.4 summarizes the design elements for a converted online course.

Course Sequence

In this example, an instructional design consultant was hired to assist the instructor one-on-one to convert the course. Instructor and consultant met initially on a weekly basis, and then monthly for six months before the course started. During consultations, the instructor reflected on the design elements of the face-to-face course by starting with objectives, outcomes, and assessments.

Table 4.4
Design Elements for a Converted Online Course

Content Type and Focus	Learning Format	Interactive Strategies	Instructor Roles	Types of Technology	Support
Group Facilitation Techniques Content-based	Self-paced and group-based	Scavenger hunt Discussion board Group project Case studies	Instructional designer Facilitator Evaluator Observer Supporter	LMS PowerPoint slides	Instructional Technical

It was then necessary to convert activities that were experiential in nature to the online environment.

Before the Course Begins   Converting a face-to-face course to the online environment requires a change in instructor mind-set. In this example, the original course involved a series of activities, and the first reaction for the instructor was to move all the activities to the online environment using different strategies to make them seem real. Comments from learners in the face-to-face course suggested that the experiential activities were the highlight of the course.

The first meeting with the consultant involved mapping the face-to-face course based on objectives, outcomes, and assessments to see how these elements were aligned. Once having completed this reflective process, the instructor realized how to equally distribute activities across course objectives, and it was easy to focus on designing the new online course. The instructor as a designer intentionally incorporated experiential face-to-face activities into the new online course; however, she eliminated some of the original activities due to redundancy.

The course design process evolved from developing the syllabus and course timeline to choosing the activities, assessments, and orientation materials. After completing the course framework, the instructor created a welcome video and letter inviting learners to access the course. This conversion process was an intense mental effort, not only in regard to redesigning the course but also because the instructor had to learn the new technology. For this instructor, working with technology was not an intuitive skill. The most challenging aspect of course design for this instructor was selecting the best medium for feedback: critiques of individual assignments left in the drop box, gradebooks, or group feedback on the discussion board. The instructor also found it difficult to structure the time spent on tasks.

During and at the End of the Course   Time spent on tasks varies from week to week depending on administrative responsibilities and due dates of assignments. Because the instructor in this example was still adapting to the technology, the first few weeks of the course were taxing. After teaching the course three separate times, she eventually developed effective strategies, such as offering the course during a more traditional 15- or 16-week semester and blocking out time for the online course, allowing for better structuring of time spent on tasks.

Instructors tend to add content and activities to a course without considering the workload and without deleting information that may not be current. During the recollection process to design this section of the course, both consultant and instructor reflected on the volume of workload and how the course could be better managed. Once the instructor in this example started exploring new activities for the experiential course, it was apparent that creating the experiential activities was not the challenge—the difficulty was in how to create a sense of presence online. During the delivery of the course, the focus was on creating presence through shared discussions and group projects.

Based on learner feedback and self-reflection, the instructor revised the converted course by minimizing redundancy and reducing the volume of activities for the next course offering. She also changed the group project into an individual activity, giving learners the flexibility to manage their own time on task. Reducing the volume of activities in a course can limit instructor workload. However, changing group projects to individual projects can increase instructor time spent on grading assignments. Table 4.5 provides a summary of managing tasks and prioritizing time for a converted online course.

Table 4.5
Managing Tasks and Prioritizing Time for a Converted Online Course

Course Sequence	Type of Tasks	Time Period/ Frequency	Estimated Time Spent
Before the course	*Design Tasks* • Convert the syllabus and course timeline • Revise readings and create PowerPoint presentations with lecture notes • Create orientation materials • Create a welcome video • Upload materials to the LMS • Activate the course in the LMS • Send a welcome letter	• 3 weeks before the course begins • 2 weeks before the course begins	• An average of 7 hours per week for 3 months (84 hours total)

(continued)

Table 4.5
(continued)

Course Sequence	Type of Tasks	Time Period/ Frequency	Estimated Time Spent
During and at the end of the course	*Administrative Tasks* • Communicate with learners through announcements • Manage the technology • Check learner participation and course interactions • Provide technical and instructional support • Respond to individual e-mails	• Weekly • Weekly as needed	• An average of 2 to 3 hours per week
	Facilitative Tasks • Ask questions during discussions, encourage participation, and solicit comments • Read learners' online posts and provide insights • Guide group activities • Share resources and solicit comments • Model icebreakers and debriefing activities	• Weekly	• An average of 4 to 5 hours per week
	Evaluative Tasks • Give group feedback • Grade assignments • Conduct midcourse feedback	• Bi-weekly • Halfway through the course	• An average of 2 to 3 hours on certain weeks

REVISING AN EXISTING ONLINE COURSE

This third example shows a revised existing online course in the discipline of education, taught by a tenured professor.

Course Tangibles

This three-credit graduate course has 25 learners who are part of an online program at a public higher education institution. This course is designed with a mixed focus on both content and process, and includes self-paced and group-based formats. Because of the course content, the level of instruction, enrollment, and the learners' connection with an established program, the instructor has chosen the following strategies for this course: group discussion, virtual teams, and concept map creation.

This instructor has taught many online courses, and he has taught this particular course more than seven times. In this course, the instructor takes on the roles of facilitator, catalyst, evaluator, and supporter. He uses the learning management system to deliver the course, and learners use concept map software to show their understanding of course concepts and to synthesize content. The instructor uploads PowerPoint slides of content and creates video announcements for each course unit, which serve as instructional support for learners. Revised orientation materials are detailed and provide technical guidance at the beginning of the course. Table 4.6 summarizes the design elements for this online course.

Table 4.6
Design Elements for an Existing Online Course

Content Type and Focus	Learning Format	Interactive Strategies	Instructor Roles	Types of Technology	Support
Distance Education for Adults	Self-paced and group-based	Discussion Virtual teams Concept map creation	Facilitator Catalyst Evaluator Supporter	LMS Concept map software PowerPoint slides Video	Instructional Technical
Content- and process-focused					

Course Sequence

It is important not to forget that for the design and delivery of an existing online course, preplanning is also needed and should start a few weeks before the course begins.

Before the Course Begins   Revising an online course can save time for the instructor, unless major modifications in content and strategies are necessary. If there are only minor modifications, such as changing dates, revising documents, redoing a welcome video announcement, or assigning learners to teams, the time spent on the design tasks can be minimal. Sending out orientation materials to learners before the course begins can diminish future workload by addressing technical and instructional issues and concerns ahead of time. In this example of an existing course, the time the instructor spent on the design tasks totaled five hours.

During and at the End of the Course   Administrative tasks are accomplished throughout the course on a weekly basis depending on the need. For example, the instructor in this instance sends out announcements with reminders and clarifications at the beginning of the course, setting the tone and expectations for the rest of the course. Once he has delivered the course multiple times, managing technology becomes an easy administrative task. In this case, problems often happen because of technology malfunctions rather than the instructor's lack of technical skills.

Learners in this course example are already part of an online program and very familiar with the technology, which reduces the number of e-mails the instructor receives. A method used to avoid the extra workload that comes with numerous questions from learners is to instruct learners to post questions in a non-content-related forum within the learning management system, where other learners can also troubleshoot issues and everyone can view the answers. The instructor is available for electronic office hours once a week via Skype, which can help him anticipate learning needs and prevent potential problems.

As a facilitator and catalyst during the course, the instructor participates in the group discussions by asking questions, encouraging contributions, sharing resources, and soliciting comments. He assigns class participants to groups of five and gives them leadership roles as facilitators and summarizers of discussions and virtual team projects. The instructor guides the team activities in the background by clarifying issues and keeping the teams focused. Instructor presence is ongoing throughout the course as he reads learners' online posts and provides insights to learners at scheduled periods, which helps him manage time and balance workload with other activities.

Evaluative tasks can be some of the most time-consuming elements of an online course; however, they play a crucial role in instructor presence. It is through individual and group feedback that learners know how they are doing in the course. Managing grading during specific times throughout the course can help balance instructor workload. In this course, the instructor provides feedback on discussion participation to individual learners at the end of each unit. Units last from two to three weeks, and a total of five units are designed for this course. The lower the number of units, the less time the instructor spends grading assignments.

Virtual team projects are set up around tasks. Learners complete short tasks throughout the semester, and immediately after each task the instructor provides feedback. At the end of the course, with all tasks completed, the final project the instructor assigns is comprehensive and well developed, and grading is minimal. Also, learners complete team and self-evaluations, which in turn reduce grading time for the instructor.

The individual assignment of creating concept maps throughout the course has a reflective component in which learners have to self-analyze their understanding of the concepts addressed in the course. Although learners each have to complete six concept maps, the reflective part of the activity makes it easy for the instructor to provide individual feedback and does not increase instructor workload because the reflection assists the instructor in more effectively understanding each concept map. An option for this assignment is to have learners complete only two concept maps, one at the beginning of the course and one at the end of the course, as a synthesis of the course concepts.

The instructor in this example conducts a midcourse feedback survey to evaluate learners' perceptions and feelings about the course up to that point. This method can be an effective opportunity to find out about learners' needs. A survey can be created through the learning management system or a third-party evaluation tool, which requires minimal work on the part of the instructor but can yield insightful feedback for course improvement.

By using time-saving strategies for existing courses, instructors can manage their workload. In this third course example, the instructor spends an average of

10 hours a week on the three-credit online course, but this amount varies from week to week. In a regular face-to-face environment, a three-credit course usually requires 45 hours of contact time throughout; the instructor meets with the learners weekly at a set time. The same amount of time is spent in this online course. The difference is the separation between the instructor and learner and the time spent on the course that spans from design (before the course) to delivery (during and at the end of the course).

By delegating and sharing leadership roles within the course, deciding in advance when to give assignment feedback, scheduling times for being online, informing learners of course expectations on a regular basis through assignment guidelines, and including team and self-evaluations, the instructor can balance workload more effectively. These strategies require organization, prioritization, and discipline on the part of the instructor. Table 4.7 provides a summary of managing tasks and prioritizing time for an existing online course.

Table 4.7
Managing Tasks and Prioritizing Time for an
Existing Online Course

Course Sequence	Type of Tasks	Time Period/ Frequency	Estimated Time Spent
Before the course	*Design Tasks* • Revise the syllabus and readings	• 3 weeks before the course begins	• 3 to 5 hours total
	• Update the course timeline • Revise orientation materials • Create a welcome video • Upload materials to the LMS • Assign learners to teams • Activate the course in the LMS • Send a welcome letter	• 2 weeks before the course begins	

Course Sequence	Type of Tasks	Time Period/ Frequency	Estimated Time Spent
During and at the end of the course	*Administrative Tasks* • Communicate with learners through announcements • Manage the technology • Check learner participation and course interactions • Provide technical and instructional support • Respond to individual e-mails	• Weekly • Weekly as needed	• An average of 2 to 3 hours per week
	Facilitative Tasks • Ask questions during discussions, encourage participation, and solicit comments • Read learners' online posts and provide insights • Guide group or team activities • Share resources and solicit comments	• Weekly	• An average of 4 to 5 hours per week
	Evaluative Tasks • Give individual and group feedback • Grade assignments • Conduct midcourse feedback	• Biweekly • Halfway through the course	• An average of 2 to 3 hours on certain weeks

SUMMARY

In this chapter we described three examples of online courses using the Template for Managing Tasks and Prioritizing Time as a point of reference. These examples addressed three different types of courses: a new online course, a course converted from face-to-face to online, and an existing online course that is being revised. The tasks were grouped based on the course sequence (before, during, and at the end of the course). When describing these tasks, we shared implications for instructor workload during the course sequence.

In Chapter Five we will expand on the four major types of workload strategies presented in Chapter One: design, support, teaching, and time allocation. Within the context of each group of strategies, we will describe approaches instructors use to manage workload and preserve quality of life.

Using Workload Strategies for Maintaining Quality of Life

*I would wake up and log on to see what [learners] had done and respond
back to them. I always had the laptop on my lap. I wondered what they
were saying. And I wanted to be in there [with them]. So workload is
more than just for the course, it's your life.*

Natalie

In the beginning of this book, we examined the online teaching
issues and challenges from institutional and instructional standpoints and discussed how these can be recognized and addressed.
Although all the issues and challenges described are important,
maintaining quality of life is essential. Personal satisfaction, control over the environment, and the ability to function in the everyday tasks of living are all characteristics of a good quality of life.
Teaching online should not interfere with one's ability to maintain
a normal and balanced life. The stories and strategies shared in this
book can help instructors manage workload and prioritize their
time as a way to find balance and success.

In the previous chapters we addressed instructional processes by providing a framework for designing an online course, identifying common tasks when teaching online, and offering the Template for Managing Tasks and Prioritizing Time. Once instructors become skilled in these processes and experienced with online teaching, managing their time should be a natural part of their workload. In this chapter we will present workload strategies that instructors can use as guidelines for their practice. We will expand on the four major types of workload strategies—design, support, teaching, and time allocation—presented in Chapter One, and will identify approaches for managing workload that correspond with each one.

DESIGN STRATEGIES

Instructors use the following design strategies to manage workload: preplanning, anticipating course responsibilities, prioritizing course activities, predicting learners' needs, and reflecting on and revising courses already taught.

Preplanning

Some examples of preplanning approaches include designing the course ahead of time and sharing the teaching load.

Designing the Course Ahead of Time   Designing the course in advance is an approach that may be time-consuming up front if the course is new, but that may result in reduced workload for the duration of the course. The outcome of the preplanning phase is a detailed syllabus, which identifies course expectations, protocols, and objectives; divides the content into units or modules; includes a course timeline; describes course activities and assessments; specifies course materials; and establishes instructor availability during the course. Once this syllabus is complete, the instructor incorporates course materials and resources into the learning management system. Some instructors may consider assigning a mandatory orientation when learners are new to the online environment. This orientation can help learners become acquainted with the learning community and assist them in acquiring specific learning skills before embarking on the online course.

For courses being converted from face-to-face to online, it is essential to plan ahead, because adapting a course requires a new mind-set and a different approach for teaching, as addressed in Chapter Four. Instructors must rethink the course and reconsider the course sequence, the types of tasks they will accomplish, the amount of time needed for tasks, and the time allocation for periods prior to and throughout the course. In a face-to-face course, instructors tend to view the course sequence from the first to the last day of class. In an online course, instructors need to view the sequence as before, during, and at the end of the course.

For online courses previously taught, but being revised, the preplanning should be less time-consuming and focus on adjusting the course timeline and modifying activities and assessments as necessary. Some learning management systems allow instructors to copy or import course materials from one course offering to another, which saves time.

Instructors can use preestablished course materials, which may reduce time for preplanning and course design. One approach for incorporating these types of materials is to base the course content on a textbook, using PowerPoint slides and a quiz bank that accompany that textbook. Another approach is to use the textbook as a foundation for the course content and supplement the course with guest speakers, podcasts, and Web links.

Sharing the Teaching Load   Sharing teaching tasks can help instructors reduce their workload. One approach is co-teaching, which includes distributing teaching tasks between two or more instructors. In this case, instructors must define their roles and responsibilities for the course and establish clear guidelines to avoid misunderstandings. Another approach is team teaching, which involves distributing design, teaching, and support tasks for the course. For example, in one team-teaching situation, several team members may work on the course design, two team members may teach the course, and one team member might provide the instructional and technical support. Again, in this situation, participants need to define roles and responsibilities and establish guidelines.

Anticipating Course Responsibilities

To manage workload, certain instructors anticipate course responsibilities, which depend on the number of jobs held, the technology being used, and when courses are offered. Instructors who teach for more than one institution often find themselves using more than one learning management system, and, because of the number of jobs held, use planning ahead as a strategy to anticipate course responsibilities. Part of planning ahead for the course is to determine course activities and assignments, as well as the date of the course's release for learners in the learning management system. In this way, the course is preset, but the instructor has the flexibility to make changes as needed.

Another approach for managing workload when employed by multiple institutions is to organize the various course materials into folders for each course. An instructor may also want to consider distinguishing among different courses in regard to online space, tasks, and time spent for each. In addition, creating a table to visually represent this distinction among courses can provide a concrete way to manage workload.

Certain instructors who anticipate heavy course responsibilities teach compressed courses during shorter terms, such as winter and summer, as a way to focus on specific academic duties. Compressed courses are more concentrated and last for a shorter period of time, thereby leaving more time for other focused work during the rest of the year. For example, for instructors who conduct research, teach, and are involved with service activities, teaching online during the summer term can help them split their time between teaching and research—and avoid the distraction of having to attend meetings to satisfy their service responsibilities while teaching simultaneously. For instructors who have administrative responsibilities in addition to teaching, anticipating administrative tasks ahead of time and placing them in a calendar can help them manage workload.

Prioritizing Course Activities

To manage workload, instructors prioritize course activities through consistency in course design, course automation features, and balanced distribution of course tasks. Having consistent design in the scope and sequence of the course units can allow for a predictable course pace. Instructors can achieve automation by using the predesigned quiz feature in the learning management system and quiz bank from the textbook. Finally, balancing course tasks among the online and other courses they are teaching can help instructors prioritize their tasks ahead of time, yet allow for flexibility during the delivery of each course.

Looking at the online course from a broad perspective, instructors are able to identify and prioritize their course tasks—and determine their time on task. One way to do this is to use the Template for Managing Tasks and Prioritizing Time introduced in Chapter Three. With this template, new or experienced instructors can identify their design, administrative, facilitative, and evaluative tasks; the time period or frequency associated with different kinds of tasks; and the estimated time spent for teaching the online course. When they teach the course again, they can revisit the template and become more efficient with their teaching.

Predicting Learners' Needs

When designing online courses, instructors who place themselves in the role of the learner can understand learners' needs and preempt problems. To do this, instructors must consider the online course design and provide a course orientation.

In designing an online course, instructors should consider creating a consistent look and feel for ease of learner access. This would include visuals, audio files, or videos to assist in content learning. Instructors might develop activities and distribute the pace of their course based on learner characteristics—traditional or nontraditional, novice or experienced with technology, native or foreign, and so on—and on their special needs.

Providing an online or optional face-to-face course orientation is a way for instructors to get to know their learners, build trust, and form a learning community. Conducting orientation activities before the course begins can serve as a support approach for predicting instructional and technical problems. These orientation activities have several purposes: they serve as icebreakers; introduce learners to the environment, the instructor, and other learners; help learners become familiar with the technology; guide learners through the course structure; help learners understand how to communicate with the group; build communities; encourage learners to share their profile information with the instructor and other learners; and introduce learners to online behavior and communication. An example of an orientation activity is the online scavenger hunt, in which learners perform a series of tasks, navigating through the course.

It is common for instructors to give access to the online course a few weeks prior to the beginning of the course so that learners can plan ahead, prioritize course activities, and be better prepared for their course responsibilities. For learners who are new to the online environment, having experienced learners share their online stories is another approach to circumvent problems.

Reflecting on and Revising Past Courses

For experienced instructors, reflecting on and revising past courses can be a strategy that helps them reduce their workload when having to teach these courses again. Some of the approaches for keeping track of their reflections include compiling notes in a notebook or a folder as the course progresses or at the end of the course, conducting midcourse evaluations, and documenting learner feedback gleaned from observations and comments. This process of reflection and feedback can help instructors become more efficient and effective in their online teaching for subsequent courses.

SUPPORT STRATEGIES

Appropriate support strategies are dependent on the instructor's level of experience in online teaching, the type of course taught, the level of the course offering, learner enrollment and needs, and the type of technology used. These strategies can involve the provision of one-on-one support, institutional support, peer support, and external support.

One-on-One Support

Instructors who are new to online teaching or are teaching sophisticated online courses may seek one-on-one support from an instructional design consultant or from staff at a teaching and learning center. One-on-one support may include intensive training, guidance in instructional design, sharing of content expertise, technology assistance, and Americans with Disabilities Act (ADA) and copyright compliance help.

Institutional Support

Instructors new to the online environment tend to avoid online teaching. Institutional support in the form of extrinsic rewards can be a motivator for instructors who are reluctant to teach online. Extrinsic motivators from the institution can include incentives (monetary support, overload pay, increased salary, a teaching assistant); rewards (release time, recognition, technology acquisition); and infrastructure support (technical assistance, administrative help).

Instructors who are experienced with teaching online often use institutional support—such as that offered by the help desk—for short-turnaround requests for assistance in designing their online courses. For courses with high enrollment, an instructor might seek institutional support by asking for a teaching assistant.

Peer Support

Some instructors rely on peer support to enhance their knowledge about and skills for teaching online, drawing on their peers' experiences to find new strategies to reduce their workload. They can accomplish this through having informal conversations, holding brown-bag discussions, observing peers' online course Web sites, and looking at course materials from colleagues to use as models or templates for their own course design.

External Support

Instructors also rely on external support in the form of resources from print materials, organizations, and Web sources. Print materials to support online courses include textbooks, journals, magazines, newspapers, and so on. Examples of organizations that can provide external support are cultural centers, historical societies, and professional associations that facilitate conferences and networking. Further, Web-based materials have become a major source of support for course development and can be easily accessed through the Internet. Nowadays instructors use YouTube, educational portals, podcasts, virtual labs, and webliographies as external support materials for their courses.

The support strategies mentioned in this book are based on our study findings and focus on workload strategies instructors consider effective. They are not meant to provide training guidelines for professional development of instructors. For comprehensive strategies for professional development, we suggest Palloff and Pratt's book (2011), which is an excellent resource for determining instructors' levels of experience, developing and delivering training directed at these levels, and building ample instructor support.

TEACHING STRATEGIES

The strategies instructors use in their online teaching, which serve as the plan of action for delivering their online courses, represent a major part of their workload. Instructors carry out tasks during and at the end of each course to meet their teaching goals. These tasks are related to administrative, facilitative, and evaluative responsibilities. In Chapter Three we explained how administrative, facilitative, and evaluative tasks affect instructor workload. We will now address approaches to carry out these tasks more efficiently and effectively in order to maintain quality of life.

Administrative Tasks

By completing administrative tasks, instructors can provide quality instruction and at the same time communicate expectations, manage the course, and support their learners. Some administrative tasks may start even before the course begins, during orientation activities with learners. These orientation activities facilitate learners' introductions to each other and the course through the exchange of personal information, informal conversations, and clarification of course expectations. During the online course delivery, administrative tasks involve communication, management, and support.

Instructors can communicate with their learners by sending weekly announcements or audio podcasts to clarify course expectations and inform them of course changes. To manage administrative tasks, they can use a calendar, the learning management system progress report, and a form to monitor learner participation. The last of these can help instructors identify individual learners when responding to e-mails and commenting on their writing. To provide additional learner support, instructors could offer specific virtual office hours and send rapid responses to e-mails. Some instructors find that they can better manage these tasks from home rather than being distracted or interrupted at work.

Facilitative Tasks

As part of completing facilitative tasks, instructors interact with learners or encourage them to interact with each other. These tasks require extended instructor engagement during the delivery of the course and involve cognitive and affective efforts (Conceição, 2006). Cognitive efforts are associated with tasks involving setting an agenda and starting a discussion, asking questions, soliciting comments, reading online posts, and sharing resources. Affective efforts include encouraging participation, providing personal insights, and guiding group or team activities. These two types of efforts often occur together in the online environment and can affect instructor workload. In this case, workload is contingent on the depth of cognitive and affective engagement with the course and learners on the part of the instructor.

To manage workload, instructors can use the following teaching strategies: limiting the number of learner posts on the discussion board or setting strict guidelines for discussions, making use of group work to share class leadership with learners, avoiding group work when there is high enrollment or there are nontraditional learners who have full-time jobs and time constraints, assigning learners to teams for project development, and involving learners in sharing new ideas for class activities. Instructors may choose to hold synchronous chats when course content requires demonstration, language skills, or participation with guest speakers.

Evaluative Tasks

Evaluative tasks that can help instructors better manage their workload are those that involve technology tools and some type of predesigned feedback approach. Technology tools, such as quizzes, surveys, and problem-solving software programs, can provide automatic grading or feedback to learners. Although instructors may spend time developing the content in the tool, time spent during the course will be minimal. Using a grading grid for reviewing online posts or grading software can also help instructors save time. In addition, they can create a file with feedback comments, and use that feedback as a foundation for personal responses to their learners.

Common feedback approaches for reducing workload are using group rather than individual grading, requiring peer grading, and giving prompt feedback to learners to avoid task overload and learner anxiety. Assigning virtual team projects can cut down on the number of final projects instructors need to grade.

For some instructors, group work may mean more work. For example, some prefer eliminating group work because learners tend to complain about collaborative work due to group conflict or time constraints. This leads to less time providing group support and helping learners resolve conflicts. In its place adding an electronically graded weekly homework application offered by the textbook publisher can reduce the amount of time in supporting learners.

For online courses that require individual grading, instructors may choose to use multiple computer screens to grade their learners' work, mainly when the assignments are text-based. Some instructors who focus on evaluative tasks rather than facilitative tasks provide in-depth individual grading and reduce their participation during group discussions.

One of the perks of teaching online is the flexibility. Instructors can teach their online courses anywhere, anytime, or any pace without being tied to a location. For instructors who travel constantly, online or hard-copy grading can travel with them. As technology rapidly changes, the ability to teach online with technology is enhanced, and many of the tasks associated with teaching a course can be accomplished with these new technologies. Learners can be unaware of instructor location and the technology the instructor is using. Location and technology become unimportant.

TIME ALLOCATION STRATEGIES

Think of an instructor traveling to a conference in China while his online course is running. He has scheduled one-on-one time with a doctoral candidate on Skype, he needs to check the discussion board for an online course, and he is pressed to provide grading feedback for another online course. He connects to the hotel wireless network in the lobby to comply with his scheduled time for the online courses. He uses the hotel room connection in the evening to link with the doctoral candidate to discuss dissertation findings. While on the plane on the way back from the conference, he uses his iPad to provide feedback on his learners' assignments. His learners have no idea where he is or what tools he is using unless he tells them. By employing technology tools in this way, instructors may feel that they are constantly connected to their courses. They may want to rethink and reconsider what really needs to be done and when. Selecting appropriate teaching strategies for managing workload, therefore, is necessary to help instructors best allocate time and find balance in their work and personal life.

Teaching online gives instructors more flexibility in terms of where and when they can work, but it can also be a trap unless they allocate their time strategically, as shown in the previous paragraph. Instructors who teach online often think that they must be ever-present for their learners. This can eventually take over instructors' other work responsibilities and personal life—a common struggle shared by many. For instructors, time allocation means controlling their time rather than having time control them. But remember that instructors are the best ones to decide what works for them.

Time allocation strategies are a necessity for online instructors. It can take between 10 to 120 hours for an instructor to design an online course for the first time. This time varies depending on the course content, support received, course enrollment, and technology used. Once the course is designed, an instructor can spend from 3 to 20 hours per week on teaching. To manage their time, instructors need to be organized and disciplined; they must distinguish between work and personal life, while simultaneously being flexible.

Being Organized

Organization is essential for managing workload because it provides structure and helps with preplanning and course delivery. Blocking out specific times for course design and delivery prior to each course is an efficient approach for time management. This can help instructors know ahead of time approximately how many hours they will spend on their online courses, and also give them more time to concentrate on actual teaching during course delivery. For some instructors, being organized can also mean being able to balance their workload more efficiently among their co-instructors and cohort groups. In addition, precourse organization helps instructors allocate time for their noncourse administrative, research, and service obligations. By carefully organizing their time, they can responsibly meet these commitments.

Organizing a course can also take the form of scheduling specific times for virtual office hours. This practice can be a time-saver in regard to answering questions and meeting learner concerns. Further, anticipating and setting aside time for periods of either heavy grading or heavy discussion can help instructors more efficiently pace their own involvement. They could avoid, for example, major work tasks during a week of extensive learner assignment feedback.

Being Disciplined

Using discipline as a method of practice can help instructors adhere to a schedule and maintain a set routine during the term of a course, and can be a time-saver in regard to workload management. Instructors who block out specific times during the day or weekend for learner responses—and stick to them—can diligently reduce their workload.

Time allocation may vary based on an instructor's work and personal life obligations. Creating routine times for work obligations might include teaching the online course according to the following blocks of time:

- Checking the online course in the early morning for two to three hours a day.

- Working on the online course from Wednesday through Sunday, because this is when learners are most often online.

- Checking the course in the early morning and late evening, leaving the rest of the day for other work or personal obligations.

- Monitoring the online course every day according to a mental checklist and closing the office door when online to prevent distractions.

- Having a lighter presence in the beginning of the week by answering general questions, and a heavier presence at the end of the week when wrapping up the discussion.

- Scheduling specific times every week on the calendar for the online course.

- Setting aside little chunks of time for the online course during the day, rather than blocking out long intervals. This strategy can help instructors keep up with the discussions, steer the discussions before any can go in a nonproductive direction, and give learners prompt feedback. For some instructors, keeping on top of things enables them to fulfill other obligations while working on the online course.

- Working on the online course every day of the week in small chunks and checking the course once on the weekend. This strategy allows for teaching anytime, anywhere, and any pace when having learners from multiple states and countries with different time zones.

Distinguishing Between Work and Personal Life

To avoid letting work take over their personal life, instructors must learn to set boundaries. Setting aside time for personal obligations is an important aspect of maintaining quality of life. Using the following strategies can help instructors maintain a healthy work-life balance:

- Working from home, in a family environment, to gain freedom to spend more time with their children and save on day care and travel-related costs.

- Avoiding working on the online course on weekends to free up time for personal matters.

- Maintaining a separate physical location for teaching online when teaching exclusively from home to allow for mental separation between work and personal life. This can enable instructors to better focus on their online courses.

- Avoiding responding to e-mails on weekends. If instructors need to write a response, they should do so, but wait to send it during regular work hours to prevent learners from expecting them to be constantly available.

- Setting boundaries by managing learner expectations through explicit communication about policies for e-mail responses and assignment feedback. Some instructors choose to respond within a specific time frame (24 to 48 hours) so that learners know exactly what to expect. Others, such as those who work in multiple positions and for different institutions, try to complete coursework when most alert and make an effort to distinguish between work and personal life.

Being Flexible

Flexibility is also important when instructors prioritize their time and manage their workload. It can allow for spontaneity when teaching opportunities arise, and can help them meet their learners' needs and accommodate their own personal issues. The key is to be prepared with a contingency plan and be open for the unexpected.

Selecting appropriate technology for online courses is one approach for creating flexibility during the course delivery. By making PowerPoint slides, developing lectures in podcasts, and selecting YouTube video resources ahead of time, instructors can concentrate on their teaching, meet learners' needs, and be spontaneous during the course delivery. Once created, these resources can be uploaded to the learning management system and may enhance time allocation flexibility for future course offerings.

Another approach that can save time is using a Word document template with examples of comments for learner assignment feedback. Instructors can simply copy and paste feedback statements matching the assignment rubric into the grading area of the course. Reusing these feedback statements can help instructors be more efficient with their time.

For process-based online courses, in which learners complete developmental tasks, instructors must be attentive and flexible as learners move throughout the course from dependence to independence in their learning. Being flexible means understanding that not all learners progress through tasks at the same pace. It also means providing learner support when needed.

Flexibility is also important in personal matters. Being flexible with oneself when personal issues arise is essential for maintaining well-being. Maybe for a period of time instructors have to rearrange their schedule to accommodate personal issues. This is okay. They must find a way to manage workload and prioritize their time to find balance and success in their personal and work life. Table 5.1 provides a summary of strategies for balancing instructor workload.

Table 5.1
Strategies for Balancing Instructor Workload

Design	Support	Teaching	Time Allocation
Preplanning	One-on-one support	Administrative tasks	Being organized
Anticipating course responsibilities	Institutional support	Facilitative tasks	Being disciplined
Prioritizing course activities	Peer support	Evaluative tasks	Distinguishing between work and personal life
Predicting learners' needs	External support		Being flexible
Reflecting on and revising past courses			

SUMMARY

In this chapter we have presented workload strategies that instructors can use as guidelines for online teaching. These strategies are based on the four major themes that emerged from our study: design strategies, support strategies, teaching strategies, and time allocation strategies. The focus of these strategies is on helping instructors determine how they can manage their workload and prioritize time in order to find balance and success in their work and personal life. In the last chapter we will offer our final thoughts and practical implications for balancing instructor workload.

Final Thoughts and Practical Implications for Balancing Workload

Widening perspectives invites openness.

The Authors

As we write this book, the number of online learners has already surpassed the total enrollment in non-online higher education programs in the United States (Allen & Seaman, 2008). This indicates that market demands are changing the educational landscape. These changes have brought benefits, limitations, and opportunities for instructors. Some of the advantages for instructors are convenience, flexibility, and increased knowledge and skills in the use of technology. Some of the disadvantages include the pressure placed on instructors to move their face-to-face courses to the online environment or create new online courses, the lack of awareness of what is involved in online instruction, and the unpreparedness of instructors who are teaching online. However, the benefits for instructors who are receptive to new opportunities and challenges can outweigh the limitations. To take advantage of these benefits, it is important for instructors to look at their teaching from an open perspective, adapt their course design, modify their workload strategies, and rethink the ways in which they can prioritize and manage their workload.

TEACHING FROM AN OPEN PERSPECTIVE

Instructors who are open to new perspectives and have ventured into online teaching have discovered that there are differences between face-to-face and online teaching in terms of workload. We can look at these differences in terms of space (tangible versus elusive), time (clear sense versus flexible concept), boundaries (specific location versus no geographical limits), the use of the senses (being able to see and hear learners and touch objects versus needing to adapt the senses and create closeness), the level of planning (spontaneously adding and adapting teaching versus preplanning), and mental and emotional efforts (having predictable time to focus the mind and emotions versus feeling constantly connected).

There are many approaches instructors must use to embark on the online venture, such as being open to these differences, staying organized, practicing discipline, distinguishing between work and personal life, and being flexible. Many of our study participants proved to be champions in these areas. Their personal stories in Chapter Two provide rich insights into their everyday work and personal experiences.

ADAPTING THE COURSE DESIGN

It is a common perception that instructors can take their face-to-face courses and simply move them to the online environment with little to no effort. However, this is a misconception. To adapt a course requires an understanding of the online teaching and learning environment, planning, and intentional design.

For a new online course, the tasks involved in designing and delivering the course will take longer than converting and revising an existing course, and will be more time-consuming. For a course converted from face-to-face to online, instructors will need to rethink how they can teach in the new environment. For revising an existing online course, they will need to revisit their tasks and time spent in order to become more efficient when teaching the course again.

Course design should be seen as an essential aspect of teaching online. Whereas in a face-to-face course instructors tend to consider teaching as extending from the first to the last day of class, an online course's duration spans from design to course delivery. Therefore, to adapt a course to the online environment, it is important to envision the "big picture." We suggest identifying course tasks and using an instructional design framework, as described in Chapter Three, as a systematic approach to guide in designing an online course. In Chapter Four we provided examples of course adaptations using our Template for Managing Tasks and Prioritizing Time.

MODIFYING WORKLOAD STRATEGIES

When instructors adapt their courses to the online environment and use a design framework to guide course development, they become aware of the differences between face-to-face and online courses, the tasks to be accomplished in the new environment, and the time span for online courses, and they realize that they have to modify their workload strategies.

This book describes four types of strategies for managing workload: design, support, teaching, and time allocation. These strategies are influenced by a variety of institutional factors, which include the type of institution, policies and procedures that guide institutional practices, the number of courses taught, enrollment, the level of instruction, the position ranking of the instructor, and infrastructure support. Depending on how these factors are combined, instructor workload is affected. In Chapter Two the instructors' stories illustrate how these factors can interact with each other and reveal the strategies instructors use to manage their workload.

RETHINKING HOW TO PRIORITIZE TIME
AND MANAGE WORKLOAD

Teaching online can be time-consuming. It involves a combination of institutional factors and requires a different type of instructional preparation. Online teaching can result in increased workload for instructors unless they are aware of what designing and delivering online instruction entail. Instructors who have not used a systematic approach to adapting their materials for the online environment tend to use workload strategies with which they are familiar, but which may not necessarily be effective or efficient. To find balance and success in online teaching, instructors need to widen their perspective, rethink their current teaching practices, and be open to new ideas.

From our standpoint, rethinking means considering current teaching practices and reconsidering them in a new light. When going through this mental process, the tendency is to reinforce old assumptions and old ways of doing things. What needs to happen is a change in mind-set—the abandonment of old assumptions about teaching and the discovery and acceptance of new ones. We suggest a four-step rethinking process.

In the process of rethinking, first instructors should examine current teaching practices by identifying course tasks (design, administrative, facilitative, and evaluative). Second, they should use an instructional design framework as a systematic approach to guide them in developing a new course or revisiting an existing one. Third, they should determine what tasks must be accomplished when designing and delivering the course, and estimate how much time might be spent for the course. Fourth, they should consider alternatives and decide on the workload strategies that will provide a balance between work and personal life.

This process of rethinking teaching practices is a dynamic one. Work and personal life are in constant motion. Instructors should revisit the online teaching process on a regular basis to find balance and success, but also remember that they are the ones who know what works best for them. See Table 6.1 for a summary of this rethinking process for prioritizing time and managing workload.

Table 6.1
Rethinking Process for Prioritizing Time and Managing Workload

Action Steps	Chapter(s) in Book
1. Look at current teaching practices by identifying course tasks.	Chapter Three
2. Use an instructional design framework to guide the design of a new course or revisit an existing one.	Chapters Three and Four
3. Determine the tasks for course design and delivery, and estimate the time these will require.	Chapters Three and Four
4. Consider alternative approaches and decide on strategies that provide balance between work and personal life.	Chapter Five

PRACTICAL IMPLICATIONS FOR BALANCING WORKLOAD

Why do instructors need to be concerned with workload when teaching online? How can instructional designers assist instructors who teach online? What can administrators in institutions of higher education do to support instructors who teach online? These are key questions that concern leaders in the field of online education and point to implications for future directions.

These questions can be answered by this book, which has practical implications for online instructors, instructional designers, administrators, and policymakers. Online instructors need to understand that their workload can have a substantial impact on their quality of life. In this book, we have provided strategies for designing, supporting, teaching, and allocating time. These strategies can help instructors prioritize time and manage their workload.

Instructional designers can play a supportive role in assisting instructors to succeed in the online environment. By understanding strategies that work best for instructors, instructional designers can help them organize, prioritize, and anticipate the various aspects of the course design process.

However, instructors need more than workload strategies and instructional designers to help them succeed in online teaching. Institutional support can serve as the foundation for instructors to embark on online teaching. Institutional leadership and management can make it happen through incentives, rewards, and infrastructure support.

Further, administrators can play a critical role in establishing, maintaining, and sustaining online offerings in institutions of higher education. They are the ones who are responsible for administrative services and infrastructure support, and are able to provide instructor incentives and rewards. By understanding instructors' workload in regard to online offerings, they can make better policy decisions and identify sound procedures for different disciplines and varying course enrollment.

Finally, this book can help policymakers who are interested in modifying the fields of distance education, instructional design, and educational technology develop guiding principles related to teaching improvement. We hope our book will influence leaders in higher education to make pragmatic changes in the field of online teaching and adequately address market demands for online learning.

Asynchronous technology: Participants do not need to be online at the same time with asynchronous technology. Information is posted and available to course participants on an anytime, anywhere, any pace basis.

Content: This determinant of presence is one influence in the creation of presence and is determined by the course discipline. A course can be process-based, content-based, or a combination of both.

Determinants of presence: These are components of the instructional design process that influence the creation of presence in the online environment. They include the type and focus of the content, the format of the learning experience, the interactive strategies implemented, the role played by the instructor, the type of technology used in the course, and the kinds of support provided.

Drop box: This is a feature of some learning management system software programs that allows users to submit assignments, eliminating the need to "snail mail," fax, or e-mail them.

Emotional presence: In this book, emotional presence relates to the ability to genuinely show feelings through words, symbols, and interactions with others in the online environment. Learners are emotionally present when they connect with others in an authentic way during the online learning experience.

Environmental experience: This is the ability to easily access and modify, provide input about, and interact with the online environment. For example, it can occur when participants have technical access and support, and have the feeling that they can affect the online environment by modifying it through challenging assumptions, providing feedback, negotiating the course design, determining team makeup, and creating and sharing projects.

Fishbowl: In this cooperative activity, learners are assigned to three separate groups: discussants, observers, and reporters. In their respective roles, each group brings an expanded perspective of a particular topic or issue.

Format: This determinant of presence is one influence in the creation of presence. The format of a course can be self-paced, group-based, or a mix of both.

Hybrid course: This is a course with a combination of face-to-face teaching and online learning.

Immersion: This happens when illusion occurs through virtual reality and individuals feel immersed in that environment. For example, when participants create avatars in Second Life®, they are immersing themselves in that virtual world.

Instructor role: This determinant of presence is one influence in the creation of presence and depends on the tasks the instructor accomplishes.

Involvement: This is the personal, interactive engagement of participants in the online environment. Designing interactive activities helps blur the line between the real and the virtual worlds. Involvement can happen during an intense online group discussion, when the conversation becomes so lively that the technology seems to disappear.

Learner progress report: This provides user log activity, such as a learner's access to specific features of the learning management system and total time spent, for either the instructor or the learner.

Learning management system (LMS):   The LMS is made up of Web-based software for delivering, tracking, and managing online courses. It also allows users to locate learning materials and activities related to online courses from any location with Internet access.

Modes of presence: These are the ways in which we experience presence.

Objective experience: An objective experience gives a sense of being psychologically and physically in another location. For example, when participants psychologically and physically are engaged in the online experience, they can feel as though the technology has become transparent and they are actually in the same room.

Perceptual presence: Perceptual presence is the sensory experience of "being there" and "being together" in the online environment. It involves the recognition of the online environment and actions in response to this environment. Through the perceptual process, which involves thought, emotion, and behavior, individuals interact with information and others and feel as though they are together in this learning experience.

Realism: Realism is present when a close match between the real world and the virtual world is created. For example, nursing simulators can provide a realistic experience of resuscitating a patient by closely resembling an actual resuscitation.

Scavenger hunt: In an online course, a scavenger hunt is a series of tasks performed online by learners, for example during the course orientation.

Sense of presence: In this book, a sense of presence is "being there" and "being together" with others throughout the teaching and learning experience. In this perspective, the instructor places the learner at the center of the online course development and creates the course for that learner. The instructor is accessible to the learners, and the learners are accessible to the instructor and each other; the technology is transparent throughout the learning process.

Social experience: This involves a sense of being with and responding to others in the online environment. It relates to the social presence derived from communicating and interacting with others or with animated characters—for example, when participants are actively interacting with each other in a discussion forum.

Strategies: This determinant of presence is one influence in the creation of presence, and it is a way of creating experiences that involve and engage the instructor with learners and learners with other learners.

Subjective experience: This type of experience relates to personal and psychological presence and takes place within one's mind. It is the illusion of being in another location. For example, when participants use the discussion board, they can have the illusion of being in another location as their minds are interacting within discussions others have posted in the online environment. This experience is unique for each person.

Support: This determinant of presence is one influence in the creation of presence and encompasses instructional and technical support. Instructional support is the psychological and emotional assistance the instructor provides to learners. Technical support is supplied to learners to help them overcome deficiencies in writing or a lack of understanding about technology.

Suspension of disbelief: Suspension of disbelief is a psychological "letting go" of reality. In this mode, the participants create the reality in their own minds. For example, when we watch a movie, read a book, or attend a drama, we "believe in" the events that are happening, even those we may never accept in the real world. We semiconsciously make a decision to put aside our real-world beliefs and accept the premise as being real for the duration of the activity. It is like living the action in the movie, book, or drama in our minds.

Synchronous technology: With synchronous technology, participants are online at the same time using real-time technology environments, such as chat rooms.

Technology: This determinant of presence is one influence in the creation of presence and involves the use of asynchronous and synchronous experiences.

Types of experience: These are the types of experience—subjective, objective, social, and environmental—inherent in the creation of a sense of presence. They are part of the Being There for the Online Learner model.

Virtual space: This is the online environment within which learners participate in the learning experience.

REFERENCES

Allen, I. E., & Seaman, J. (2008). *Staying the course: Online education in the United States.* Newburyport, MA: Sloan Consortium.

Andersen, K. M., & Avery, M. D. (2008). Faculty teaching time: A comparison of Web-based and face-to-face graduate nursing courses. *International Journal of Nursing Education Scholarship, 5*(1), 1–12.

Betts, K. S. (1998, October). Why do faculty participate in distance education? *The Technology Source.* http://technologysource.org/article/why_do_faculty_participate_in_distance_education/.

Bower, B. (2001). Distance education: Facing the faculty challenge. *Online Journal of Distance Learning Administration, 2*(1), 1–6.

Carnevale, D. (2004). Professors seek compensation for online courses. *Chronicle of Higher Education, 50*(49), A27. http://chronicle.com/weekly/v50/i49/49a02701.htm.

Carroll-Barefield, A., Smith, S. P., Prince, L. H., & Campbell, C. A. (2005). Transitioning from brick and mortar to online: A faculty perspective. *Online Journal of Distance Learning Administration, 8*(1). www.westga.edu/~distance/ojdla/spring81/carroll81.htm.

Conceição, S.C.O. (2006). Faculty lived experiences in the online environment. *Adult Education Quarterly, 57*(1), 1–20.

Conceição, S.C.O., & Lehman, R. M. (2010, September). *Faculty strategies for balancing workload when teaching online.* Proceedings of the Midwest Research-to-Practice Conference in Adult, Continuing, and Community Education, Lansing, Michigan. www.msu.edu/~mwr2p/ConceicaoLehman-MR2P-2010.pdf.

Conceição, S.C.O., & Schmidt, S. (2010). How non-content-related forums influence social presence in the online learning environment. *Indian Journal of Open Learning, 19*(2), 73–85.

DiBiase, D. (2000). Is distance teaching more work or less work? *American Journal of Distance Education, 14*(3), 6–20.

DiBiase, D. (2004). The impact of increasing enrollment on faculty workload and student satisfaction over time. *Journal of Asynchronous Learning Networks, 8*(2), 45–60.

DiBiase, D., & Rademacher, H. (2005). Scaling up: Faculty workload, class size, and student satisfaction in a distance learning course on geographic information sciences. *Journal of Geography in Higher Education, 29*(1), 139–158.

DiSalvio, P. (2007). Revising workload, promotion, and tenure policies for online faculty. *Distance Education Report, 18*(11), 4–8.

Dunlap, J. C. (2005). Workload reduction in online courses: Getting some shuteye. *Performance and Improvement, 44*(5), 18–25.

Dykman, C. A., & Davis, C. K. (2008). Online education forum: Part two—teaching online versus teaching conventionally. *Journal of Information Systems Education, 19*(2), 157–164.

Ehrlich, T. (2003). The credit hour and faculty instructional workload. *New Directions for Higher Education, 2003*(122), 45–55.

Euben, D. (2003, October 5–7). *Lives in the balance: Compensation, workloads and program implications.* Paper presented at the 13th annual Legal Issues in Higher Education Conference, Burlington, VT.

Lehman, R. M., & Conceição, S.C.O. (2010). *Creating a sense of presence in online teaching: How to "be there" for distance learners.* San Francisco: Jossey-Bass.

Lorenzetti, J. P. (2007). Setting boundaries: Four tips for managing your time online and not letting your work consume your life. *Distance Education Report, 11*(15), 1–2, 7.

Maguire, L. (2005). Literature review—Faculty participation in online distance education: Barriers and motivators. *Online Journal of Distance Learning Administration, 8*(1), 1–16.

Miller, M. T., & Husmann, D. E. (1999, Fall). Faculty incentives to participate in distance education. *Michigan Community College Journal, 5,* 35–42.

Moore, M. G. (2000). Editorial: Is distance teaching more work or less? *American Journal of Distance Education, 14*(3), 1–5.

Mupinga, D. M., & Maughan, G. R. (2008, Winter). Web-based instruction and community college faculty workload. *College Teaching, 56*(1), 17–21.

O'Quinn, L., & Corry, M. (2002). Factors that deter faculty from participating in distance education. *Online Journal of Distance Learning Administration, 5*(4), 1–16.

Palloff, K. M., & Pratt, K. (2011). The excellent online instructor: Strategies for professional development. San Francisco: Jossey-Bass.

Scheuermann, M. E. (2005, January). Course quality and instructor workload: Pt. 1. *Distance Education Report, 9*(1), 4–7.

Sheridan, R. (2006). Reducing the online instructor's workload. *Educause Quarterly, 3*(11), 65–67.

Thompson, M. M. (2004). Faculty self-study research project: Examining the online workload. *Journal of Asynchronous Learning Networks, 8*(3), 84–88.

Visser, J. (2000). Faculty work in developing and teaching Web-based distance courses: A case study of time and effort. *American Journal of Distance Education, 14*(3), 21–32.

Wilson, C. (1998). Concerns of instructors delivering distance learning via the WWW. *Online Journal of Distance Learning Administration, 1*(3). www.westga.edu/~distance/wilson13.html.

Zuckweiler, K. M., Schniederjans, M. J., & Ball, D. A. (2004). Methodologies to determine class sizes for fair faculty work load in Web courses. *International Journal of Distance Education Technologies, 2*(2), 46–59.

INDEX

A

Administrative tasks: identifying, 51, 53, 62; office hours, 33, 43, 91; required for new online courses, 65, 68; for revised existing online courses, 76; simplifying, 88

Allen, I.E., 1–3, 95

American Journal of Distance Education, 13

Andersen, K.M., 3, 13

Asynchronous technology, 44, 45, 60, 101

Avery, M.D., 3, 13

B

Balancing workload. *See* Workload

Ball, D.A., 3, 10, 15

Being There for the Online Learner model, 55, 56

Betts, K.S., 3, 14

Blocking course time: case study in, 21, 29–30; discipline required for, 91–92; during initial course period, 41–42; to most productive hours, 39, 40, 43

Boundary setting: allocating time for online courses, 30; choosing to provide 24/7 commitment, 27, 28, 68; communicating to learners, 27; distinguishing between work and

personal life, 92–93; for instructors in multiple positions, 42–44; limiting discussion board postings per week, 47, 89; strategies for setting, 23; teaching from home and, 35–36. *See also* Blocking course time; Quality of life

Bower, B., 3

C

Campbell, C.A., 6, 8, 11

Carnevale, D., 3

Carroll-Barefield, A., 6, 8, 11

Case study stories: about, 19–20; advantages of experience in managing workload, 36–38; blocking time for online course, 28–30; co-teaching, 20–23; cohort program as time-saver, 40–42; handling current topics courses, 45–48; home-based teaching, 34–36; managing time, rather than time managing you, 27–28; parameters for authors', 15–17; planning ahead to balance workload, 23–25; recurring mixed-mode online courses, 44–45; scheduling short-term instruction, 30–32; strategies for giving individual feedback, 25–27;

task management for multiple courses, 42–44; teaching for multiple institutions, 32–34, 38–39

Classrooms: comparing online and traditional, 50; virtual space, 104

Co-teaching: balancing workload with, 20–23; case study in, 20–23; mixed-mode online courses using, 44–45; quality of life enhanced by, 83, 91

Cohort programs: balancing workload with, 91; case study in, 20, 40–42

Collaborative strategies, 59

Colleges. *See* Institutions

Communications: types of course, 51

Conceição, S.C.O., 1, 7, 11–13, 16, 52, 54, 88

Content, 101

Content-based courses, 57

Converting face-to-face courses: course sequencing when, 71–74; design elements for converted courses, 71; redeveloping into online courses, 38–39, 49–50, 96–97; tangibles for, 70–71

Cooperative strategies, 58–59

Corry, M., 3, 4–5, 10

Courses: accounting for workload using metric system, 7; allocating time for design and delivery of, 12–14, 15; anticipating learner's needs in, 85; anticipating responsibilities of, 83–84; converting face-to-face, 70–74; creating new online, 64–70; demand for online, 6; designing ahead of time, 82–83; developing blueprint for, 52–53; identifying tasks of, 51–52; issues and challenges, 9–15; online vs. face-to-face, 11–12, 13, 20; preventing confusion when teaching multiple, 39; prioritizing activities for, 84–85; process-based and content-based, 56–57; quality of, 8, 37;

revising existing online, 74–79, 85–86; self-paced, 57; size of, 10; transitioning face-to-face to online format, 38–39, 49–50, 96–97. *See also* Converting face-to-face courses; Creating new courses; Revising existing online courses

Creating a Sense of Presence in Online Teaching (Lehman & Conceição), 54, 61

Creating new courses: administrative tasks required for, 65, 68; course tangibles and design elements, 64, 65; defining course sequencing, 65, 68–70; design tasks for building, 65, 66–67; managing tasks and prioritizing time for, 69–70

Current-topics driven courses, 21, 46

D

Davis, C.K., 3

Design elements: for converted courses, 71; for new online courses, 64, 65; for revised existing online courses, 75

Design strategies: allocating course time, 12–14, 15, 29; co-teaching, 20, 22; creating cohort program as time-saver, 40; giving individual feedback, 25; handling current topics courses, 46; identifying course tasks, 51–52; managing workload based on experience, 20, 36–37; planning ahead to balance workload, 23–24; preparing recurring mixed-mode online courses, 44; pressures to create online course, 2; providing sense of instructor presence, 54–61; strategies for, 16; supporting quality of life, 82–86; teaching for multiple institutions, 32–33; teaching online during short terms, 31, 84. *See also* Design strategies; Design tasks

Design tasks: identifying for course, 51–52, 62; required for new online, 65, 66–67

Determinants of presence, 101

DiBase, D., 3, 7, 13

DiSalvio, P., 3, 7

Discussion forums: limiting discussion board postings per week, 47, 89; monitoring, 47; sharing assignments among group in, 26

Drop box, 101

Dunlap, J.C., 3

Dykman, C.A., 3

E

Emotional presence, 101

Environmental experience, 101–102

Erhlich, T., 7

Euben, D., 7

Evaluative tasks: managing for quality of life, 89–90; quizzes, 26, 31, 35; for revised existing online courses, 77; types of, 52, 53, 62. *See also* Feedback

Evaluators, 59

Experience: applied to workload management, 20, 36–37; environmental, 101–102; objective, 103; social, 103; subjective, 104; types of, 104

External instructor resources, 87

F

Face-to-face instruction: difference in online vs., 11–12; offering orientation to online course as, 24; redeveloping into online format, 38–39, 49–50, 96–97; teaching times for online vs., 13, 20; workloads combining online and, 28–29. *See also* Converting face-to-face courses

Facilitative tasks: identifying, 51–52, 53, 62; simplifying, 88–89

Feedback: managing to fit workload, 89; soliciting course, 37; strategies for giving individual, 20, 25–27; supportive, 61; time required for, 68. *See also* Grading

Fishbowl, 102

Flexibility for instructors, 90–91, 93–94

Flow charts, 54

Format: defined, 102; impact on presence, 57; redeveloping course into online, 38–39, 49–50, 96–97

G

Grading: allocating time for, 43; making more efficient, 26, 89; providing feedback on performance during, 61; using online gradebook, 35

Group-based courses, 57

Groups: evaluating time required for, 89; forming learner, 22; limiting discussion board postings per week, 47, 89; saving time with, 41; sharing assignments in discussion forums, 26

Guest speakers, 46

Guilt, 68

H

Help desk, 27

Home-based teaching case study, 21, 34–36

Husmann, D.E., 3

Hybrid course, 102

I

Immersion, 102

Independent study courses, 29

Infrastructure of online teaching, 10–11

Institutions: defining and recognizing workload requirements, 6–7; growth of online teaching at, 1–2; infrastructure support of, 10–11; new perspectives on online learning, 5–6; online teaching issues for, 3–8; practical implications of workloads for, 99; providing online instructor support, 86; reexamining concept of workload, 6; teaching for multiple, 21, 32–34, 38–39

Instruction: instructional strategies, 58; instructional support, 60; issues and challenges of online, 9–15; learner-centered, 56; teaching from new perspectives, 96. *See also* Courses; Face-to-face instruction

Instructor-led strategies, 57–58

Instructor role, 102

Instructors: acquiring new perspectives on, 5–6; administrative support for online, 5; anticipating responsibilities of courses, 83–84; challenges managing workload, 2–3; co-teaching, 83, 91; co-teaching with, 20–23; connecting with online learners, 2; developing online presence, 54–61; distinguishing between work and personal life, 92–93; flexibility for, 90–91, 93–94; implications of balanced workloads for, 99; maintaining quality of life, 81–82; modifying online workload strategies, 97; one-on-one support for, 86; online vs. traditional interactions of, 50; openness to new perspectives, 96; peer support for, 87; predicting needs of learners, 85; pressures to design online courses, 2; providing 24/7 commitment, 27, 28, 68; quality-of-life factors for online, 14–15, 42; responding to e-mails, 24, 27, 29–30, 37, 41; rethinking priorities and workload, 97–98; roles in online teaching, 59; sharing course leadership, 45, 76, 78; skepticism of online instruction, 35; summary of workload stories by, 21; supporting

learners, 60–61; teaching assistants for, 25, 86; tracking course progress for future classes, 38. *See also* Presence; Quality of life

Involvement, 102

L

Labs for online courses, 35, 63, 66, 86

Learner-centered instruction, 56

Learner progress report, 102

Learner-shared leadership roles, 45, 76, 78

Learners: accommodating pace of, 93; connecting online teaching to, 2; course differences for online vs. face-to-face, 11–12, 50; creating sense of presence for, 54–61; establishing communication with, 15; growth in online, 1–2; helping them plan ahead, 40; increasing number of online, 95; involving in own learning, 24; new perspectives on, 5–6; predicting needs of, 85; teaching nontraditional, 23, 38–39

Learning: gaining new perspectives on online, 5–6; involving learners in own, 24; modular, 40; paradigm shift in online, 4–5

Learning management systems (LMS): communicating via, 26; defined, 102; keeping up with different, 32–33; teaching with variety of, 33

Lehman, R.M., 11, 12, 14, 16, 54, 61

Logistical strategies, 58

Lorenzetti, J.P., 3

M

Maguire, L., 2, 3, 5

Maughan, G.R., 2, 7

Mentors, 34, 59

Miller, M.T., 3
Mixed-mode online courses, 21, 44–45
Modes of presence, 102
Modular learning, 40
Moore, M.G., 10
Mupinga, D.M., 2, 7

N

Nontraditional learners: planning to meet needs of, 23; teaching, 38–39

O

Objective experience, 103
Office hours: setting online, 33, 91; taking questions during, 43
One-on-one support, 86
Online teaching: allocating design and delivery time for, 12–14, 15; authors' study of, 15–17; demand for online courses, 6; differences in, 11–12; growth of, 1–2; instructional challenges for, 9–15; issues for institutions, 3–8; market demands for, 3–5; paradigm shift in online learning, 4–5; presence in, 12; providing quizzes, 26, 31, 35; quality of life and, 14–15; time required for face-to-face vs., 13, 20; work and effort required for, 7. *See also* Presence
O'Quinn, L., 3, 4–5, 10
Organizing work, 91
Overload, 39

P

Palloff, K.M., 15, 87
Peer support, 87
Perceptual presence, 103
Personal life, 92–93
Planning ahead: balancing workload by, 24; case study about, 21, 23–25; helpful design strategies for, 82–86; multiple institutional roles necessitating, 32–34;

preplanning and designing courses, 32–34, 39–40
Podcasts, 37, 46
Pratt, K., 15, 87
Presence: about online, 12; content determining, 56–57; creating sense of, 2; determinants of, 101; emotional, 101; establishing, 47; format's impact on, 57; instructor role and online, 59; learners lessening need for instructor, 35; maintaining daily, 28; modes of, 102; perceptual, 103; responding to e-mails, 24, 27, 29–30, 37, 41; staying constantly connected, 43; strategies role in, 57–59; types of online support, 60–61
Prince, L.H., 6, 8, 11
Priorities: developing for course activities, 84–85; rethinking time, 97–98; setting for new courses, 69–70. *See also* Template for Managing Tasks and Prioritizing Time
Process-based courses, 56–57
Productivity: instructors' fears about, 10

Q

Quality of course, 8, 37
Quality of life: design strategies supporting, 82–86; enhancing by co-teaching, 83; factors in online teaching, 14–15, 42, 68; handling administrative tasks to simplify, 88; instructor flexibility and, 90–91, 93–94; maintaining, 81–82; managing evaluative tasks for, 89–90; peer support for instructors, 87; providing one-on-one support for instructors, 86; simplifying facilitative tasks, 88–89; support strategies enhancing, 86–87; teaching strategies enhancing, 87–90; time allocation strategies allowing, 90–91, 94

Quizzes: grading and preparing, 31; preplanning, 35; providing for courses, 26

R

Rademacher, H., 7

Realism, 103

Recurring mixed-mode online courses, 21, 44–45

Research: dedicating time for, 31, 32

Responses: to e-mails, 24, 27, 29–30, 37; reflecting on, 41

Rethinking priorities and workload, 97–98

Revising existing online courses: course sequencing when, 76–79; delegating and sharing leadership roles, 78; maintaining quality of life by, 85–86; preplanning times when, 83; tangibles for, 75; tasks and priorities for, 74–79

Rewards for online teaching, 10, 15

S

Scavenger hunt, 103

Scheuermann, M.E., 3

Schmidt, S., 58

Schnierderjans, M.J., 3, 10, 15

Scripts, 54

Seaman, J., 1, 2, 3, 95

Self-discipline, 91–92

Self-paced courses, 57

Sense of presence, 103

Sequencing course tasks, 65, 68–70, 71–74, 76–79

Sheriden, R., 3

Short-term online teaching: balancing workload with, 84; case study in, 21, 30–32

Smith, S.P., 6, 8, 11

Social experience, 103

Software programs: designing course templates in, 54

Stories. *See* Case study stories

Storyboards, 54

Strategies: defined, 103

Students. *See* Learners

Subjective experience, 104

Support, 104

Support strategies: co-teaching, 22; cohort programs as, 40–41, 91; defined, 16; enhancing quality of life, 86–87; giving individual feedback as strategy, 25; handling current topics courses, 46–47; managing time, rather than time managing you, 27; providing Web resources, 87; scheduling short-term courses, 31, 84; teaching for multiple institutions, 38–39; time blocking as, 29; types of online, 60–61

Supporters, 59

Synchronous technologies, 60, 104

Systems thinking paradigm, 3–5

T

Tasks: administrative, 51, 53, 62; design, 51–52, 62, 65, 66–67; evaluative, 52, 53, 62; facilitative, 51–52, 53, 62; managing for multiple courses, 21, 42–44; prioritizing course activities, 84–85; sequencing course preparation, 65, 68–70, 71–74, 76–79; templates for managing, 61–62.

Teachers. *See* Instructors

Teaching. *See* Instruction

Teaching assistants, 25, 86

Teaching strategies: blocking time for online course, 29–30; co-teaching, 22; creating cohort program as time-saver, 41; defined, 16; designing short-term courses, 31, 84; enhancing quality of life, 87–90; experience managing workload, 37; giving individual feedback as strategy, 26; handling current topics courses, 47; managing time, rather than time managing you, 28; planning ahead to balance workload, 24; preparing recurring mixed-mode online courses, 44–45; teaching for multiple institutions, 39; when teaching for multiple institutions, 32

Technical support, 60

Technology: adapting to online, 68–69; asynchronous, 44, 45, 60, 101; selecting time-saving, 93; synchronous, 60, 104. *See also* Learning management systems

Template for Managing Tasks and Prioritizing Time: converting face-to-face courses, 73–74; for existing online courses, 78–89; managing tasks with, 61–62; new online courses, 69–70

Templates for learner feedback, 26

Thompson, M.M., 1, 3

Time allocation strategies: about, 16–17; blocking time for online course, 30, 39, 40; case study in, 21, 27–28; co-teaching, 22; creating cohort program as time-saver, 41–42; defined, 16–17; defining course sequencing, 65, 68–70, 71–74, 76–79; developing for course design and delivery, 12–14, 15; effect of experience on, 37; flexibility for instructors, 90–91, 93–94; giving individual feedback as strategy, 26–27; handling current topics courses, 47; managing time, rather than time managing you, 28; needed for feedback task, 68; planning ahead to balance workload, 24; preparing recurring mixed-mode online courses, 44–45; rethinking time priorities, 97–98; teaching for multiple institutions, 33, 39; teaching online during short terms, 31, 84. *See also* Blocking course time

Timelines, 54

Traveling, 90

Tutors, 59

Types of experience, 104

U

Universities. *See* Institutions

V

Videoconferencing strategies, 44–45

Virtual space, 104

Visser, J., 13

W

Web resources: supporting instructors with, 87; using and providing, 46–47

Wilson, C., 2–3, 13

Workload: balancing instructor's role with, 59; challenges managing, 2–3; co-teaching and, 20–23; defining institutional practices for, 6–7; design strategies balancing, 82–86; implications for balancing, 99; managing feedback to fit, 25–27, 89; modifying strategies for online, 97; organizing time to manage, 91; perception of online, 2; planning ahead to balance, 23–25; program quality and instructor, 8; reexamining concept of, 6; rethinking management techniques for, 97–98; sequencing course tasks, 65, 68–70, 71–74, 76–79; types of strategies for, 16–17, 94. *See also* Case study stories; Quality of life

Y

YouTube videos, 31, 37, 93

Z

Zuckweiler, K.M., 3, 10, 15

More Resources from the Jossey-Bass Online Teaching and Learning Series!

The Essential Online Teaching and Learning Tool Kit
ISBN: 1118027213 | Price: $105.00 USD

Online teaching and learning is expanding rapidly on campuses everywhere, yet educators often lack the resources they need to translate their courses to an online environment. We've taken the guesswork out of assembling the professional development library you need, offering hand-picked resources that cover all of your online teaching and learning needs.

Tool kit includes:

Learning In Real Time by Jonathan E. Finkelstein

Engaging the Online Learner by Rita-Marie Conrad and J. Ana Donaldson

Assessing the Online Learner by Rena M. Palloff and Keith Pratt

Conquering the Content by Robin M. Smith

Creating a Sense of Presence Online by Rosemary M. Lehman and Simone C. O. Conceicao

---

Join The Jossey-Bass Online Teaching and Learning Community!

The Jossey-Bass Online Teaching and Learning (OTL) Conference ONLINE
Based on the popular series of Jossey-Bass guide-books on online teaching and learning, the OTL Conference Online brings all of the books' authors – as well as a community of hundreds of professionals worldwide – right to your desktop for interactive online sessions, discussions, hands-on learning, strategy swapping, and networking. The conference takes place every October, so mark your calendars in advance!

The Jossey-Bass OTL Community Website
The learning continues all year round at the Jossey-Bass OTL community website. You'll be the first to know about details of the upcoming OTL conference, receive information on the newest professional development resources from Jossey-Bass, learn about the latest free podcasts and video clips from your favorite authors and experts, and discover much more! You can also sign up for the *OTL Update*, a FREE monthly e-newsletter full of the latest tips and tricks from experts in the field – just visit the site and sign up today!

Join our community and be the first to know about the final dates and details of our next OTL Conference Online by visiting **www.onlineteachingandlearning.com**.